Peter Haining has been an admirer of the Spitfire all his life. He lives in East Anglia with his wife and three children, near several of the bases from which the Spitfire squadrons set forth during the Second World War.

D1579331

THE
SPITFIRE
LOG

A Tribute
to The World's Most Famous
Fighter Plane

COMPILED BY
Peter Haining

Futura

A Futura Book

Copyright © 1985 by Peter Haining

First published in Great Britain in 1985 by Souvenir Press Ltd
Reprinted 1986 and 1989
This edition first published in Great Britain in 1990 by Futura Publications,
a Division of Macdonald & Co (Publishers) Ltd, London & Sydney

ISBN 0 7088 4438 3

Typeset by 🅰 Tek Art Ltd, Croydon
Printed and bound in Great Britain by BPCC Hazell Books Ltd
Member of BPCC Ltd, Aylesbury, Bucks, England

Futura Publications
A Division of
Macdonald & Co (Publishers) Ltd
66–73 Shoe Lane
London EC4P 4AB
A member of Maxwell Pergamom
Publishing Corporation plc

Acknowledgements

The author would like to thank the following publishers,
magazines and agencies for permission to use their material
in this book: Associated Newspapers, *Horizon* magazine,
Chatto & Windus, *The Daily Telegraph*, Ziff-Davis Publishers, Methuen, *The Sunday Times*, *Life* magazine, *Aeroplane* magazine, *Punch*, *The Times*, *The Royal Air Force
Review*, *The Daily Express*, John Murray (Publishers), Air
Ministry Records Office, the Imperial War Museum, the
British Museum, the British Newspaper Library, the BBC
Sound Archives, Messrs Vickers Ltd. The photographs are
from the author's own collection.

Contents

For
My Father
who lived this magnificent era

The Men Who Made the Spitfire

March 6, 1936, was a typical early Spring day in England. A covering of high, grey clouds had remained virtually unbroken since dawn and, in the far south of the country, there was a light wind blowing in from the English Channel across Southampton. On the outskirts of this town, at Eastleigh Aerodrome, a small group of men were gathered around a sleek, elegant single-seater aircraft with a fixed-pitch airscrew and stub exhausts. It was painted in a pale blue enamel and its only markings were the registration letters K5054.

At first glance, it might have seemed like any other day at this industrious little airport beside the River Itchen, a mile or two from its junction with Southampton Water and the appropriately named River Test. There was the noise of engines running, the sound of mechanics busy inside the various hangars, and the intermittent take-off and landing of small aircraft.

But the little group of men, all employees of the Vickers Supermarine Aircraft Company were, in fact, about to witness a piece of aeronautical history. For, exactly 50 years ago this year, that privileged group saw a legend born.

At the centre of the group stood a big, thick-set man, Flying Officer Joseph Summers, known to one and all by the nickname 'Mutt'. Despite his size, 'Mutt' Summers was renowned for his amazingly quick reactions and his exceptional natural talent as a pilot. Friends had been known to say of him that you could 'fix a propeller to a kitchen table' and he could fly it, and he himself admitted that he flew planes more by the seat of his pants than by instruments. Yet even airmen who were sticklers for 'doing it by the book', and disapproved of his intuitive way of flying, were of the opinion that he was probably the leading test pilot of his generation.

Certainly 'Mutt' had an impressive background. Born in London in 1904, he had as a child become fascinated by the exploits of the World War I pilots, and eagerly joined the Royal Flying Corps as soon as he was old enough. He spent five years at Martlesham Heath near Ipswich, which since 1916 had been the official Aeroplane and Armament Experimental Establishment. Here he had proved himself an outstanding pilot, at a centre which had earned itself a reputation for the most accurate and thorough testing of new aircraft. Indeed, it was said that a 'Martlesham Report' could not be bettered for comprehensiveness and impressive weight of detail, while a Martlesham pilot could fly anything a designer wanted to put into the air. Standards were, quite simply, higher than anywhere else – and the pilots were also, beyond question, the very best.

In 1929, however, 'Mutt' Summers had resigned his commission and left Martlesham on being offered the job of chief test pilot at Vickers, as replacement for 'Tiny' Schofield, tragically killed in an accident. Despite the fact that there were perhaps elements of his flying not in the Martlesham tradition, 'Mutt's' individualistic style was precisely what Vickers required for their various high-speed prototypes. From that year on, he was the pilot who first took up any new aircraft.

Summers' size was matched by his personality – outgoing and ebullient, he enjoyed not only the challenge of the test flights, but also the excitement and glamour that went with them. Unlike many of his contemporaries, 'Mutt' did not shrink from publicity, and revelled in the awe in which he was widely held. When he flew anything other than single-seater machines, observers who went along with him returned with breathless tales of his ability. These admirers said that you could tell just what a good test pilot he was simply by the look of his mouth and his knuckles when he was in the air.

Standing beside Summers as he prepared to climb into the pale blue prototype was a thin, sandy-haired, rather stooped man, his florid face drawn with an inner pain he was obviously doing his best to conceal. He was Reginald Joseph Mitchell, known as 'R.J.', an aeroplane designer of undoubted genius who was about to watch the fulfilment of a dream. For the prototype was his – at that moment quite untried, but destined to make his name immortal, and in time to play a major part in saving his generation from one of the most hideous tyrannies that ever set out to enslave mankind.

Born in Stoke-on-Trent in 1895, R.J. Mitchell had reached this moment of destiny through a mixture of sheer hard work and an obsession with machines. As a youngster he had been a voracious reader of books on engineering, ships, cars and planes, and at the Wedgwood Institute in Burslem had won the Midland Counties Union prize for mathematics. Apprenticed to a locomotive works, he continued to study in the evenings and within a year had become an assistant engineer. That was in 1915, and although he volunteered for the Royal Flying Corps, his firm categorically refused to release him.

However, such was his growing fascination with aircraft that in 1917 he left the locomotive shops for the Supermarine Aviation Works, where he got a job as a draughtsman. Here he had really begun to develop his talent for designing, and in the years which followed had helped to create the revolutionary streamlined monoplanes which dominated the prestigious Schneider Trophy contest. But looking beyond them, Mitchell had also dreamed of a land-based fighter machine. Now, on this blustery March day, his dream was about to become a reality.

There was, however, an anxiety plaguing Mitchell even more deeply than the cancer which he already knew was inexorably killing him. For he could foresee an aerial menace to his beloved Britain–and desperately wanted to provide the fighter that could match and overcome this threat. All his waning energies had been devoted to this end, and every day for months past he had been present in the Eastleigh workshops as his drawings were translated into fact.

As Mitchell paced about the rather ramshackle workshops, he watched the mechanics build a small, clean fuselage and add to it slim, curved wings. Nothing escaped his eagle eye, and whenever a problem arose, he would retire to his office, cup his face in his hands, rest his elbows on the drawing board, and ponder the dilemma for hours until it was solved. No one in the workshop resented his presence or even his occasional interruptions: the men, too, had the feeling they were building something powerful, graceful and uniquely important.

Another of the men grouped around the prototype was suffering a similar agony–though from anticipation rather than any physical pain. He was Ken Scales, the foreman who had been in charge of the building of the aeroplane. Rarely absent from the workshops throughout the entire construction, he could smile with pride at the finished product which had been rolled from the hangar onto the runway. Many a prototype had come this way in the past, Ken Scales could not help thinking, but had there ever been one so *vital* before?

For not far over the other side of the English Channel a man named Hitler had risen to power, and by his massive rearmament was giving evidence of a desire for

10

conquest. His army was poised to annex the Rhineland and his airforce, the Luftwaffe, had already relegated Britain to a mere fifth position in the ranking of air powers. It was now time, perceptive people like Scales believed, for England to arm herself against what they saw as inevitable conflict with Germany.

But it had required more than a little good fortune for this small band of men gathered on a March morning to have been able to create this jewel among aeroplanes.

After receiving some last minute instructions and making the final checks, 'Mutt' Summers swung himself up onto the prototype's wing and slid into the narrow cockpit. He closed the perspex canopy, fastened his parachute and Sutton harness, primed and started the Rolls Royce Merlin engine, and with a wink at the group of people now moving back from the aircraft, rolled the machine forward.

According to a somewhat glamorised version of this historic moment, the plane then taxied off westwards across the big grass airfield, and moments later 'shot forward like an arrow from a bow and left the ground after an incredibly short run.' Folding up its wheels, it climbed mesmerically upwards, according to observers, and was soon lost from view. Summers was also said to have been carried away by the excitement, so the story goes, and was 'inspired with such confidence that he showed off a little of what the plane could do in the way of banks and turns.' When he landed his first words were supposedly an ecstatic, 'I don't want anything touched!'

The truth is, however, just a little more prosaic. Now, although the first impressions of a test pilot *are* of crucial importance–and in the case of such an astute man as Summers, with his uncanny habit of being right, they are doubly so–the plane did not take to the air perfect in every respect: the flight *was* purposely simple and short, and alterations *were* required.

We have the precise facts on record from another of the

men on the ground, Jeffrey Quill, a slight and rather reserved 23 year-old former RAF pilot of exceptional skill, whom Summers had just recently persuaded to join him at Vickers as an assistant. Not long after this flight, Quill was himself to take over the testing of the prototype, but no recollection remained stronger in his mind than that of the first flight.

'There was a light wind blowing across the aerodrome,' he says, 'which meant that "Mutt" had to take the short run, and he taxied towards one of the four large Chance lights which (in those days) were situated round the perimeter, turned into the wind and opened the throttle. The aeroplane was airborne after a very short run and climbed away comfortably. "Mutt" did not retract the undercarriage on that first flight–deliberately, of course– but cruised around fairly gently for some minutes, checking the lowering of the flaps and the slow flying and stalling characteristics, and then brought K5054 in to land.'

Summers taxied towards the hangar, where the anxious party of Supermarine employees were waiting, says Quill, who goes on to dispel another popular illusion about what happened next.

'When "Mutt" shut down the engine,' he recalls, 'and everybody crowded round the cockpit, with "R.J." foremost, "Mutt" pulled of his helmet and said firmly, "I don't want anything touched." This was destined to become a widely misinterpreted remark. What he meant was that there were no snags which required correction or adjustment before he flew the aircraft again. The remark has crept into folklore implying that the aeroplane was perfect in every respect from the moment of its first flight– an obviously absurd and impracticable idea.'

There was, however, no denying that 'Mutt' Summers was delighted with the new plane: as were Mitchell, Scales and all the other members of the Vickers team. The pale blue fighter had all the appearance of a thoroughbred, and though there was still much to be done before it would be wholly serviceable, its character and effectiveness were there for all to see. All it really lacked at the moment was a name . . .

As can be surmised, this remarkable plane was the natural outcome of a series of events that could actually be traced back to the very infancy of aeronautics–to 1909, in fact, and the work of one of the earliest pioneers, Noel Billing. This former seaman, Boer War veteran and yacht chandler, had begun experimenting with the idea of flying boats in that year, and also opened a workshop by the Floating Bridge at Southampton. He called the place the Supermarine Works.

Here, Noel Billing built a succession of ingenious marine craft until the outbreak of the First World War, which necessitated his joining the Royal Naval Air Service. At this, the Supermarine Works passed into the hands of another brilliant young man, Hubert Paine, who, with a mixture of astute management and the employment of talented designers and engineers, made the firm a power in the land. Among these men was R. J. Mitchell, who by 1920 had become the number one designer.

In 1922, the adventurous Paine financed a British entry to try and win the Schneider Trophy, a contest run annually since 1913 by the Fédération Internationale Aéronautique to find the fastest seaplane. As the rules said that the first country to win the Trophy three times in succession, or four times in all, kept the coveted prize, Paine knew it was a do-or-die endeavour, for the Italians had won the two previous years' contests.

The talent of R. J. Mitchell was brought to bear on this challenge, and in Naples his creation was unveiled–the superbly streamlined Supermarine Sea Lion II Flying Boat with a powerful 450 mph Napier Lion engine. The machine was a revelation: until then aeroplanes had been bi-planes of wood and plywood. Mitchell's entry with its bullet-like fuselage perched high above huge floats and with a *single* wing, not to mention streamlining, was irresistible. It won handsomely–pushing the record speed up by almost 30 mph to 145.7 mph.

At this juncture Hubert Paine left Supermarine, and Vickers became the proprietors. The Americans, too, decided to challenge for the prestigious Trophy, and at Cowes in 1923 it was snatched away from under the Brits' very noses by a Curtis Navy Racer. There was no contest in 1924, but the following year, in Baltimore, the Americans were winners again, and it was only the intervention of the Italians, with a Macchi 39, in 1926, that prevented a US hat-trick.

But while these two nations had been locked in friendly rivalry, and Italy was once again on the verge of a final triumph, R. J. Mitchell had not been idle. In 1927 he presented his new design, the Supermarine S5, and at Venice, piloted by Flight Lieutenant Webster of the RAF, it snatched back the initiative with a new record speed of 281.656 mph. The following year, Mitchell produced a bigger version, the S6 with a 12-cylinder Rolls Royce engine replacing the Napier Lion. With Flying Officer H. R. D. Waghorn in the cockpit it, too, was a convincing winner over the Spithead course, at 328.63 mph.

However, the very next year, with the elusive hat-trick of victories within reach, disaster very nearly overtook Mitchell's Supermarine. Despite the two previous victories, the Air Ministry decided not to finance another plane–and nor was the British aircraft industry interested in sponsoring a high-speed seaplane. Winning was all very well, they said, but what *practical* application did it have? A huge public outcry greeted this announcement, but no amount of pressure could make the authorities change their minds.

Then, after two more years with no contest, a saviour unexpectedly appeared in the form of the eccentric millionairess, Lady Lucy Houston. Determined that this opportunity should not be lost, she offered a donation of

14

£100,000 for the building of a new machine.

Time, unfortunately, was against the creation of an entirely new plane, but Mitchell and his team worked feverishly against the clock to reward the old lady's generosity and the public's faith. In under six months they had radically modified the existing S6 with new floats and cooling circuits to enable the giant Rolls Royce engines to run at full throttle during the entire race; and on an emotion-packed September day in 1931, the Supermarine entry triumphed for the third successive time. The Schneider Trophy was Britain's for ever. As if to crown the success, a few weeks later Flight Lieutenant George Stainforth pushed the existing world speed record up to 407.5 mph, becoming the first human being to travel in excess of the magical 400 mph mark, and also setting a record which was to stand for 14 years!

The end of the race also marked the end of Mitchell's absorption in seaplanes. But within a matter of months, the Air Ministry was inviting manufacturers to come up with designs for a new single-seat fighter plane for the RAF. The specifications, however, were very exacting.

At Supermarine, Mitchell seized upon this new challenge with all his usual energy–after all, designing a fighter plane had been one of his dreams since childhood– but from the very outset of the official restrictions made the task seemingly impossible. Still, he produced a gull-winged prototype, designated the S7/30, and from February, 1934, 'Mutt' Summers flew it, on and off, for several months. But the plane was not a success. It proved too big for its power–the steam-cooled Rolls Royce Goshawk engine could only manage a top speed of 230 mph. It clearly had no operational future.

Mitchell, and Supermarine, had no alternative but to shelve the plans: and into obscurity went the S7/30. Only the name by which it had been called was destined to survive–the 'Spitfire'.

There was no turning Mitchell from his dream,

however, and his employers, sensing that he was on the way towards achieving something quite unique, decided to give him *carte blanche* in seeking to create a more successful alternative plane. And as a result of being freed from bureaucratic restrictions, he gave birth to the K5054. It was everything he had worked towards, and his pleasure was there for all to see on that windy March day half a century ago. Even his nagging pain was temporarily forgotten.

If there was even so much as a minor irritation for Mitchell, it came two months later when he was informed that the Air Ministry–who were delighted with the new plane–had decided on a name for it. They were going to revive the name of its ill-fated predecessor, 'Spitfire'.

'The sort of bloody silly name they *would* give it', was all he could bring himself to mutter. For once, of course, he was quite wrong.

Silly name or not, the Spitfire was soon being put through an extensive series of tests, primarily at Martlesham, where 'Mutt' Summers and later Jeffrey Quill methodically proved its capabilities. And in the June of that same year, the sheer genius of Mitchell's idea was underlined when the Air Ministry placed an order for 310 of the Spitfire Mark Is–it was the single largest such order ever given to a manufacturer.

For the technically minded, the specifications of the single-engined fighter were these: length, 29 feet 11 inches; wing span 36 feet 10 inches; engine, one Rolls Royce Merlin II Vee-type; maximum speed, 362 mph at 18,000 feet; operational ceiling 31,900 feet; range, 395 miles; armament, eight 0.303 Browning machine guns.

Tragically, though, R. J. Mitchell himself did not live to see a single one of the production Spitfires flown, although he must have been well aware that his plane was a good one. Just *how* good he would never know. After struggling courageously against the cancer which he refused to allow to interfere with his work, he died on

June 11, 1937. He was just 42 years old.

'Few men have been more deeply mourned by those with whom and among whom they worked,' air historian C. G. Grey wrote shortly afterwards. 'He was always ready to stand up to his seniors if he thought that their views or their decisions were wrong. And he was equally willing to listen to the suggestions of his juniors. I know of nobody who worked under Mitchell who did not love and respect him. I do not know what kind of monument can be raised to his memory, but he has the greatest monument that any man can have: he lives in the memories of those among whom and for whom he worked–that is to say, the officers and men of the Royal Air Force.'

In fact, of course, he had already won a degree of fame because of his success in the Schneider Trophy contests, but this became rapidly more widespread once the public began to hear of the Spitfire. The plane made its first public appearance at the RAF display at Hendon on June 18, 1936, later flying over the crowds at the SBAC display that same weekend. Billed as 'the world's fastest fighter', its reception was instantaneous and rapturous. This proved, however, just a small step towards Mitchell's greatest triumph, when the 'Spit' acquitted itself so magnificently during the Battle of Britain a few years later.

The plane also proved itself one of the most enduring of all fighter aircraft: for not only was it to be the only fighter on the Allied side to remain in full production throughout the entire Second World War (going through continuous modification, gaining 2,000 lb in weight and increasing its speed by nearly one hundred miles per hour), but it was still being manufactured until 1948, and was not finally taken out of front-line RAF service until 1951. All told, over 20,000 Spitfires were built, between them winning a victory which ranks with the greatest battles in our history, as well as creating a legend which will surely last as long as aircraft continue to take to the skies.

If there is a secret to the Spitfire's success, it is surely the basic soundness and brilliance of Mitchell's original concept that made it such a versatile machine. And though 'R.J.' may not have been enamoured of the name fate chose to bestow upon it, that, too, undoubtedly had a significant part in the success, as one of its most famous pilots, Group Captain Sir Douglas Bader, was to remark years later. 'Spitfire,' he said, 'was a name that resounded round the free world in those dark years of Hitler's tyranny, and perfectly symbolised the mood of Britain's defiance.'

In the years since its début, the plane has won admirers in every corner of the earth, first from the pilots who flew it during the war years–as well as those who flew *against* it–and since then from aeronautical experts of every shade of opinion.

For instance, one anonymous English pilot, waxing lyrical, said, 'You feel like Henry the Fifth in armour and Joan of Arc tied to the stake at the same time. You can move your hands, feet and head the few inches that are required; your Spitfire will do the rest. You are the most powerful, the fastest, the most manœuvrable fighting man in the world.'

Perhaps a little less colourful, but still as deeply felt, are those words of the great French air ace, Pierre Closter-mann, who wrote reflectively a few years ago, 'For a pilot every plane has its own personality, which always reflects that of its designers and colours the mentality of those who take it into action. The Spitfire, for instance, is typically British. Temperate, a perfect compromise of all the qualities required of a fighter, ideally suited to its task of defence. An essentially reasonable piece of machinery, conceived by cool, precise brains and built by conscien-tious hands. The Spitfire left such an imprint on those who flew it that when they changed to other types they found

18

it very hard to get acclimatised.'

It is also true, of course, that the Spitfire was very much a plane of its time, arriving at the very moment when its capabilities as a fighter were just what was required for the war about to burst upon Europe. It was indeed with a certain justification that another air historian, David Masters, could write in his book, *So Few*, published in 1941, that 'future historians may state with some degree of truth that when Great Britain won the Schneider Trophy, she really won the war which saved Civilisation.'

The Spitfire has, with every reason, earned a special place in aviation history as well as in the hearts of ordinary men and women, not just because it symbolised a nation's hopes for freedom, but because it flew so superbly and came close to embodying the kind of grace and elegance that mankind has so admired in the birds since the dawn of history. In a way, it was our dreams given wings–and even in our present age of supersonic missiles and space travel, there is much to respect in the feat of design and engineering which it represents.

Today we may fly higher, further and faster, but the Spitfire may just have given its pilots the closest feeling to that of being like a bird. And a ferocious bird of prey, to be sure! No wonder a whole generation of young men found it their highest aspiration and greatest pride to be a Spitfire pilot.

Perhaps the one frustrating thing about the plane, however, is the feeling that, because the Spitfire was a single seater, only those who actually flew in it can fully appreciate the magic. As that pilot-turned-bestselling-author, Gavin Lyall, has so perceptively noted, 'With such a–relatively–small number actually experiencing aerial warfare, it is difficult to find first-hand accounts. In too many famous actions, particularly towards the beginning of the war, hardly anybody survived to tell the personal story. And in any case, you cannot fit a war correspondent into a Spitfire.'

Yet a few of 'The Few' did survive, if in some cases only long enough to record in the very briefest terms their thoughts and impressions. Some merely wrote factual reports, others kept diaries, and a few actually produced articles and essays. There were just a handful of books, too. A fortunate few of these men are still alive today to tell the tale of those days in the air–which they do with the kind of self-deprecating modesty which marks all of their kind. And so, to commemorate the Spitfire's 50th birthday, I have talked to some of these survivors, as well as locating some of the diaries and articles of those not so fortunate. From their deeply-felt experiences, I present this tribute to the noblest of fighter planes.

I offer it as a personal tribute, too, for as a child growing up in the war-torn Britain of the early 1940s, I vividly recall standing transfixed and unaware of danger in the garden of our home at Enfield, watching a Spitfire pursuing a German 'Flying Bomb' close overhead. As my mother gathered me up and ran indoors, I heard the dull thump of an explosion not too far off. Later–much later– I was to learn that the Spitfire pilot had used the wing of his plane in a dangerous manœuvre to tip the Bomb off its course and force it to plunge harmlessly onto a stretch of farmland. Without that unknown aviator's skill, that 'Doodle Bug' might well have landed in the heart of our neighbourhood–and I might not today be writing these words.

So in memory of all those who paid the ultimate price so that we might enjoy our freedom half a century on, *The Spitfire Log* celebrates a glorious chapter in aviation history: a chapter the like of which I doubt we shall ever experience again.

Peter Haining
March 6, 1985

Specifications of the Spitfire

Because of the advent of the Second World War not long after the development of the Spitfire, it was some time before any kind of technical data about the plane was released to the public. The specialist journal, *The Aeroplane,* carried the first precise information in the following article, published, appropriately, in the month of March, 1941.

The Spitfire is of straightforward stressed-skin design. The elliptical cantilever low wing, which tapers in thickness, is built upon a single spar with tubular flanges and a plate web. Forward of the spar, the wing is covered with a heavy-gauge light-alloy sheet which forms the torsion box with the spar. Aft of the spar, the covering is of thinner gauge sheet with light-alloy girder ribs. The wing spars are detachable for ease of maintenance and repair. Split flaps are between the ailerons and the fuselage.

The fuselage is an all-metal monocoque, built on four main longerons with transverse frames and a flush-riveted light-alloy skin. The front frame forms the fireproof bulkhead and is built as an integral part with the centre portion of the main wing spar. To help in maintenance the tail portion of the fuselage with fin and tailplane is detachable.

The tail unit is of the cantilever monoplane type. The fin is integral with the rear fuselage. The tailplane is of metal with smooth metal covering. The elevator and rudders have light-alloy frames and fabric covering. There are trimming tabs on elevator and rudder.

The undercarriage is fully retractable outwards into the under surface of the wings. There are two Vickers cantilever oleo-pneumatic shock absorber legs which are retracted hydraulically. An emergency hand system is fitted to lower the wheels should the hydraulic system be damaged.

The first Spitfire had a tail skid, but the production models have a fully castoring tail wheel which does not retract.

The Rolls Royce Merlin II 12-cylinder Vee liquid-cooled motor when operating on 87 octane is rated at 990 hp at 12,250 feet, and has a maximum output of 1,030 hp at 16,250 feet and for take-off. The forward-facing intake effect gives a top speed at a rather greater height. The motor is slung in a steel tube mounting.

The radiator, which is fully ducted to give low drag by low velocity cooling, is in a duct underneath the starboard wing with a hinged flap for temperature control. The oil tank of 55 gallons' capacity is underneath the engine with its surface forming part of the body contour.

There are two fuel tanks with a total of 85 imperial gallons' capacity in the fuselage in front of the pilot. Feed is direct to the engine through fuel pumps. There is an electric starter and hand turning gear.

The enclosed cockpit is set over the wings with a sliding canopy and hinged panel in the fuselage for entry and exit.

The armament is eight Browning guns mounted in the wings, four on each side of the fuselage. Access to them, for inspection and maintenance, is through doors in the top and bottom surface of the wings.

A camera gun is also installed and has proved of use in showing details of fights with enemy aeroplanes. There is full radio installation, electrical, night-flying and blind-flying equipment.

*   *   *

(It will be noticed that no mention is given here of the top speed of the Spitfire: at the time the article was published, this information was still classified.)

Eight Guns for a Fighter

Air Marshal Sir Ralph Sorley, the Controller of Research and Development in the Ministry of Aircraft Production from 1943 to 1945, explains from his unique viewpoint how the Spitfire was evolved and armed.

As the individual who was (I think without controversy) responsible for the original eight-gun fighter concept, I should like to put on record the sequence of events, so that in times to come there will be no ambiguity as to how or why the Spitfire and the Hurricane became the conquerors they were in 1940 and remained the finest fighter aircraft during much of the rest of the 1940–45 war.

My posting to the Air Staff Department (OR) which was responsible for evolving the operational requirements for new type aircraft, armament and various other equipment, occurred early in 1933. Disarmament was the order of the day, and the Royal Air Force, in common with the other Services, was being cut to the bone. Fantastic limitations were being set to the size of ships and aircraft, above which we were not to be allowed to build. For instance, our heavy bombers must be limited by international agreement to an all-up weight of 16,000 lb, it was said. A study of our intelligence information about the progress being made in Germany and other countries pointed to a disregard of the hampering restrictions which we were trying to obey. It seemed inevitable that war with Germany would come sooner or later, and, unless we could get out some new requirements in time, we should be surpassed and would be too late.

During 1933 my whole waking hours were devoted to the one problem: what fighter could be evolved which would stand the highest chance of defeating the fast bomber? Our fighter force had been brought to a high standard of training on the biplane. Its low wing loading had for years been regarded as the first essential for manœuvre in attack. The monoplane was suspect on the grounds of strength during aerobatics and rigidity as a gun platform. Most fighter opinion favoured the biplane. But now the monoplane bomber began to show such an advantage in performance when fitted with retractable undercarriage, flaps, and, later, the variable-pitch propeller, that only another monoplane would be comparable. It seemed inevitable that, whatever the aerobatic advantages of the biplane, it would no longer catch the bomber, and so a monoplane it must be. And it must have all the new features of retractable undercarriage, enclosed cockpit, flaps, etc., in order to make it as fast as possible and so give the pilot his chance of catching his enemy. Now, how to kill?

Like so many others, I had spent many years trying to hit targets with one, two, or even four machine-guns, with, I confess, singularly poor results. Others were so much better, but I estimated that, if one could hold the sight on for longer than two seconds, that was better than average. We were now going to have to hold it on at appreciably higher speeds, so the average might even be less than two seconds. The two or four-gunned biplanes had been equipped with Vickers guns in general, the residue of vast stocks left over from the 1914–18 war. By 1934 a new Browning gun was at last being tested in Britain which offered a higher rate of fire. After much arithmetic and burning of midnight oil, I reached the answer of eight guns as being the number required to give a lethal dose in two seconds of fire. I reckoned that the bomber's speed would probably be such as to allow the pursuing fighter only one chance of attack, so it must be destroyed in that vital two-second burst.

Before deciding to specify eight .303 machine-guns, I gained access to the Hispano-Suiza Company in France and in great secrecy learnt something of their development of a 20 mm gun. In the bowels of a fort near Paris we saw this gun in action, and its destructive power was most impressive. For accuracy it required such a rigid mounting I despaired of finding such a degree of stiffness in a monoplane wing, and so for the time being that weapon had to be discarded. Later, as soon as the stiffness of the Hurricane wing had proved itself in practice, two and four-gun 20 mm installations were proposed, and I commenced that step during 1935. Nevertheless, the development of the gun, ammunition feed, and mountings took several years, and it was late 1940 before a reliable installation in both Hurricane and Spitfire was ready for service.

The Vickers guns had always been installed in the fighter's cockpit, within reach of the pilot, so that, should the guns jam (as they frequently did), he could, by great dexterity and exertion with a wooden mallet, clear the jam and resume the battle. This also meant restricting the rate of fire to synchronize the firing with the position of the propeller blades in relation to the gun muzzles. My calculations showed it necessary to build up a density of bullets which would be lethal over almost any part of the target aircraft, but to do that the Browning rate of fire must be the maximum. For that reason, but not that alone, the guns must be clear of the propeller, and, therefore, the wings seemed the obvious place. But the density of bullet pattern would depend on the rigidity of the wing. The high aerodynamic performance demanded of such aircraft required both strength and rigidity of the wings, and should, therefore, be sufficient for the small-calibre guns. That placed four guns each as two batteries in either wing, but well off the centre line of sighting for the pilot–yet another departure from the orthodox. The guns being well away from the pilot, it also meant a new method of firing the guns. Fighter pilots had used the simple Bowden wire and thumb-press lever on the control column, but now we needed instantaneous firing of all eight guns at the exact moment, and the Bowden wire was replaced by a pneumatic system.

Throughout 1933 I discussed these features with my friends, and at last felt satisfied with the thinking; the concept was right, but it was built up on rather a lot of imagination and would produce a totally different fighter from anything the fighter pilots were accustomed to. I was cautious, therefore, where I discussed these ideas in the early stages, for fear of arousing reaction too soon; and to obtain confirmation I arranged with a Major Thompson, who had helped me so much over the Browning gun data, that we would obtain an obsolete aircraft, set it up on a range, mount eight guns at 400 yards, fire bursts of two seconds with solid and explosive ammunition, and assess what happened. This we did on the ranges at Shoebury, and to my joy the effect was all I had imagined. The structure was cut through in so many vulnerable places that one could safely count on two seconds as being the necessary lethal dose. With that bit of evidence behind me, I think the specification F5/34 came out in the open, and many meetings were held where, finally, unorthodoxy carried the day.

It was about then, I believe, I confessed to Dowding that I had borrowed one of his old aircraft and shot it to ribbons, and it must have been about then that he said he had previously authorized Major Buchanan, his Director of Technical Development, to place orders for two purely experimental monoplanes to allow their designers to try out all the new features–retractable undercarriage, etc.–which I had envisaged would be necessary. An experimental development such as this by DTD would not necessarily originate from Air Staff departments, and I certainly did not know before then that these aircraft were being built.

Thus, by coincidence, both Camm and Mitchell were well away on the aircraft, but up to that point their hitting power was quite a secondary consideration. They were presumed to be capable of mounting four orthodox guns firing through the propeller. I soon was busy convincing Camm and Mitchell of the vital necessity of building the eight-gun concept into their designs, and, from that moment, I had their willing and enthusiastic support and cooperation. Camm's aircraft presented a somewhat easier problem than Mitchell's because of the essential difference in their designs. The Hurricane had a very thick wing which made the mounting of the wing batteries relatively easy, but Mitchell held out for a relatively thin wing, and so the guns had to be mounted separately over the whole span. Nevertheless, he was keen to do it; indeed, in both aircraft the fuselage was reduced in cross-sectional area, and thereby gained in performance, as a result of the change. After a while new sets of wings were ordered which were delivered after the first flights of the prototypes, and one can truly say that was the evolution of the Hurricane and Spitfire as the eight-gun fighters as we know them.

As an insurance the Gloster Aircraft Company were given an order for an eight-gun fighter to specification 5/34 with a Bristol air-cooled engine. (The Hurricane and Spitfire were both designed around the Rolls Royce Merlin.) These two aircraft were then given specification numbers F36/34 and F37/34, which brought them into line with the 5/34. I have copies of all the relevant documents. It is true that Mitchell had build a previous monoplane to the F7/30 specification–a monoplane with a cranked, thick wing and fixed undercarriage–and I am not surprised he did not think much of it. It was neither one thing nor the other.

It was confirmed much later by my old friend Orlebar, who commanded Fighter Development Unit, that the principle of the lethal burst was effective; but it rests everlastingly with the pilots of Fighter and other Commands to size it all up in those very few words one frequently heard whenever they spoke of the heat and burden of their day–'Oh, I just gave him a squirt.'

A Flight to Remember

Air Vice Marshal James 'Johnnie' Johnson, one of the top
Allied fighter aces of the Second World War and arguably
the most famous pilot ever to have flown a Spitfire, recalls
his eventful first encounter with the plane which was to
change his life . . .

The day I flew a Spitfire for the first time was one to
remember. To begin with the instructor walked me round
the lean fighter plane, drab in its war coat of grey and
green camouflage paint, and explained the flight-control
system. Afterwards I climbed into the cockpit while he
stood on the wing root and explained the functions of the
various controls. I was oppressed by the narrow cockpit
for I am reasonably wide across the shoulders and when
I sat on the parachute each forearm rubbed uncomfortably on the metal sides.

'Bit tight across the shoulders for me?' I inquired.

'You'll soon get used to it,' he replied. 'Surprising how
small you can get when one of those yellow-nosed brutes
is on your tail. You'll keep your head down then! And get
a stiff neck from looking behind. Otherwise you won't last
long!'–and with this boost to my morale we pressed on
with the lesson. After a further half-hour spent memoriz-
ing the various emergency procedures and the handling
characteristics, the instructor checked my harness straps

and watched while I adjusted the leather flying-helmet.

'Start her up!'

I carried out the correct drill and the Merlin sprang into life with its usual song of power, a sound no fighter pilot will easily forget. The instructor bellowed into my ear:

'You're trimmed for take-off. Don't forget your fine pitch, otherwise you'll never get off the ground. Good luck.' And he ambled away with a nonchalant air, but I knew that he would watch my take-off and landing with critical eyes.

I trundled awkwardly over the grass surface swinging the Spitfire from side to side with brakes and bursts of throttle. This business was very necessary for the long, high nose of the aircraft made direct forward vision impossible and more than one pupil had recently collided with other Spitfires or petrol bowsers. I reached the very edge of the airfield, and before turning into wind carried out a final cockpit check. No aircraft was in sight on the circuit and I had the whole airfield to myself. I swung her nose into the wind. No more delays now, get off. Throttle gently but firmly open to about four pounds of boost. She accelerates very quickly, much faster than the Master. Stick forward to lift the tail and get a good airflow over the elevators. Correct a tendency to swing with coarse rudder. No more bouncing about. We can't be airborne yet! Yes, we are, and already climbing into the sky. Things move fast in the Spitfire! Wheels up. Pitch control back and throttle set to give a climbing speed of 200 mph. Close the hood. After a struggle, during which the nose rose and fell like the flight of a magpie, I closed the perspex canopy and the cockpit seemed even more restricted than before. I toyed with the idea of flying with the hood open, but I could not fly or fight at high altitudes in this fashion and I must get acquainted with every feature of the plane.

Now it was time to take a firm hand with this little thoroughbred, for so far she had been the dominant partner in our enterprise. I carried out an easy turn and tried to pick up my bearings. Not more than four or five minutes since take-off, but already we were more than twenty miles from Hawarden. I flew back, gaining confidence with every second. A Master looms ahead and slightly below. I overtake him comfortably, and to demonstrate my superiority attempt an upward roll. I forget to allow for the heavy nose of the Spitfire with sufficient forward movement of the stick and we barrel out of the manœuvre, losing an undignified amount of height. Better concentrate on the handling characteristics and leave the aerobatics for another day. Over Hawarden again. Throttle back to a circuit speed. Hood open. All clear ahead. Wheels down and curve her across the wind. Now the flaps and a final turn into wind. 120 mph on the approach and we are too high. Throttle back and she drops like a stone. 100 mph and over the boundary. Stick back and head over the side to judge the landing. Too high and in a semi-stalled condition we drop out of the sky to hit the unyielding ground with a hefty smack. As I suspected, my instructor had seen it all and was there when I switched off the engine.

'I saw the Spit get you into the air! And given a fair chance she would have carried out a better landing than yours! If you make a mess of your approach, open up and go round again. You've been told that with every plane you've flown. Get into the front seat of that Master and I'll show you a Spitfire circuit.'

To be relegated back to the second team, as it were, was a severe jolt to my pride.

'Right, I've got her, Johnson. We're on the downward leg. The Spit is heavier than the Master and soon loses height when you cut the power. So make your circuit tight and try to get a steady, continuous turn from here. It looks good. You're down quickly, and if you're turning you can watch the sky behind. Remember that when you're down south, for you're a sitting duck on the circuit!

Wheels down and adjust the trim. Flaps down. Continue the turn. Now into wind. Plenty of height–perhaps a little too much so we sideslip a bit off–so! Throttle right back. Ease back the stick and check her. She's sinking. Stick right back and she's down. Piece of cake, isn't it?'

Four days later I made a mess of the approach, but this time with disastrous results. I had been instructed to land at Sealand and deliver a small parcel of maps which were stuffed into my flying-boot. The circuit at Sealand was crowded with Masters and I weaved amongst them for a favourable into-wind position. There was a stiff wind across the short, grass airfield and I aimed to be down close to the boundary fence so that I had the maximum distance for the landing run. I came over the fence too high and too slow and the fully stalled Spitfire dropped like a bomb. We hit the ground with a mighty crash and I had a little too much slack in the harness straps, for I was thrown violently forward and pulled up with a nasty wrench across the shoulders. For a few yards we tore a deep groove in the ground, then she slithered to a standstill in a ground loop which tore off one undercarriage leg and forced the other through the top of the port mainplane. I switched off the petrol cocks and the ignition switches and stepped out. The duty officer, an immaculate flight lieutenant complete with webbing and revolver, stepped out of a car and eyed me coldly:

'It was quite apparent you were going to prang. You were too high, too slow, not enough power, a poor approach . . .' And so on. 'Don't you know the country's short of Spitfires? What do you want here anyway?'

'I was told to deliver these,' I replied. And handed him the maps.

I found my way back to Hawarden and reported the dismal facts to the flight commander. He was a good type and made allowances for the fact that I was trying to get into a short airfield. He had me airborne in another Spitfire very shortly afterwards and I heard no more of the accident. But I was suspect and knew that my flying was watched closely. Another prang and I would certainly be washed-out.

One of The Few

Pilot Officer Eric Marrs, a 20 year-old fighter pilot with No. 152 Squadron, kept a personal diary of the Battle of Britain until his death in July, 1941. These early entries vividly capture the days leading up to the terrible conflict in the skies.

March 26, 1940
I have flown at last. On Friday I went off in a Gladiator without any other dual instruction. It is a very easy machine to fly and handles something like the Hinds which I have just been flying. When I have done a certain number of hours on this type I shall go on to Spitfires, and then I shall have to do a number of hours on Spitfires before I become operational on them. I have done about four hours on Gladiators since I started and I like them very much. They are very nippy and manœuvrable and are easy to land. Their top speed is supposed to be about 250 mph . . . Life is quite interesting on the whole, but it ought to liven up soon if the Germans are going to do anything at all.

April 2
I have got onto Spitfires at last. I had my first trip on Sunday and it was rather hectic. They are very sensitive and delicate on the controls at low speeds and after the

other aeroplanes I have been flying I found myself being very ham-handed with the controls. Apart from this, they are very nice machines. The view forwards and downwards is not too good but is otherwise excellent, though when coming into land the approach is made with the nose up, and that makes you very blind. A special curving approach is thus necessary, which only leaves you blind for the final hold off. The speed is not noticeable until you get near the ground. On the whole they are very gentlemanly aircraft and the only really bad habit is a tendency to tip up on to its nose very easily, on the ground. This necessitates great care in using the brakes . . . There has been very little excitement here and we are all longing for the sight of a Hun.

April 14
I am getting on quite well with the Spitfire and have begun learning the methods of attack. These we practise in sections of three on one or three aircraft flying in a steady, straight line. It would be much more amusing if we had a bomber at our disposal on which to practise these attacks, while it did its best to evade us. The bombers, however, have more serious work to do.

April 21
I am nearly up to operational standard on Spitfires having done about 10½ hours on them. Even when one is operational one gets plenty of training and practice flying, and as the Hun seems to be too preoccupied with Norway to do anything about Britain I expect to get in a good deal more practice before I have to fly in earnest.

May 15
Our sector still remains deadly quiet, though we are all at an advanced state of preparedness and ready for anything. I am taking my part in day operations now and have been off on one chase. We were sent about 50 miles out to sea

but saw nothing. When you start going out to sea like that, it makes you listen very carefully to your engine.

I have also started night flying. Spitfires are very nice at night as they are very stable machines and can be trimmed to fly hands and feet off. We also have to get up very early to be at readiness an hour before dawn; this works out that we get up at 3.30 about four mornings out of six, and if you have been night flying the night before it means that you get about 1½ to 2 hours' sleep some nights. It is surprising though with what little sleep one can do when the need arises. Besides, our work is not at the moment strenuous . . .

May 29
I think our squadron will move soon; in fact I am nearly sure it will move soon. We will not be leaving this sector unguarded for another squadron will move in. The Southern squadrons, however, cannot carry on indefinitely and our job will be to relieve one of them for a spell. We are supposed to be next on the list for either France or South of England, from where we will guard the evacuation of the BEF or escort bombers.

When the system really gets going there will be a continous rotation of squadrons to and from the battle area.

June 9
We were left out of the Dunkerque show and have been stuck up here all the time, and very quiet it has been, too. Still, we're bound to be given action some time and the war won't end yet awhile.

July 7
We have at last been having some work to do these nights, but up to now only two bombers have been shot down in our sector. One by anti-aircraft fire and the other by the other squadron. On Friday night we had a proper go at

them. There was, however, a general over-excitement of the ground defences, and the searchlights and guns were not up to much. Most of our own fighters were fired on and some had a bad time. The guns did, however, get their one enemy aircraft that night. They also received a large and powerful raspberry for firing on us. I was not actually on duty that night, but was aerodrome control pilot and was out on the flare-path all the time. The next three nights they did not visit us again. On the fourth night my flight was on again and I went up this time. The guns and searchlights were, however, too shy this time and they never even picked up a friendly aeroplane, much less an enemy one. We searched and patrolled and did what we could, but unless the searchlights illuminate aircraft for us we are not much use. The next day we had a big conference with the searchlight officers from all the sectors round and cleared up many points and questions. That night the other squadron was on. The searchlights were a 100 per cent better and they fixed on a Hun which was promptly shot down. We now feel that with good co-operation between searchlights and fighters we can do fairly well. That happened last night. Tonight we are on again, but it is the other flight's turn . . .

July 19
Our squadron had another little engagement some days ago. They came up against some Ju 87s escorted by Me 109s and with a Do 17 as a decoy. I say they because I was unfortunately at breakfast during this show and missed it. They shot down the Do 17, a Ju 87 and the two Me 109s confirmed, with one or two others rather doubtful. We had one pilot, Jumbo, shot down, but he got out all right with a leg wound and was picked up from the sea shortly afterwards. Since then things have been very quiet indeed round here. The Germans seem to be concentrating chiefly round Dover and Folkestone at the moment. Probably because that is the narrowest part of

the Channel. The raiders that we have to deal with come, I think, from the Channel Island aerodrome at Jersey. We often fly more than halfway across and see France quite clearly. The other day one section chased an enemy machine right over to France before they gave up . . .

I Fought in the Sky over Dunkirk

Pilot Officer John Allen was another young fighter pilot, but unlike Eric Marrs was actually involved in the magnificent rescue of the British troops from Dunkirk in May, 1940. Two months after giving the following eyewitness account of the battle–for which he was awarded a DFC–Allen was reported 'killed in action while flying in operations against the enemy'.

We got a 'stand by' early in the morning of the first day of the Dunkirk evacuation, and at 9 a.m. we got our orders. There were twelve of us, and climbing to 20,000 feet we headed across the North Sea. I don't remember many personal impressions of that first journey out, except the feeling that here was something really doing at last. You must remember that for many weeks we had carried out offensive patrols up to the French and Belgian coastline, but had never seen any Huns. I remember being slightly worried about my engine, but somehow in a single engine one always has slight quirks of mind about the motor when one is flying over the sea, perhaps it is the difference in the sound that does it.

We kept well together, but of course kept radio silence. We knew every inch of the coastline to which we were heading, but even without that knowledge there was no mistaking it was Dunkirk. Only a few minutes after leaving Britain and at our height we could see the pillars of smoke arising from the burning town and the villages all the way up from Calais. The horizon was one vast pall. We went right across the city and settled down to patrolling on a 50 mile-long beat, but we saw nothing and decided to come downstairs.

At 4,000 feet we were beetling along still looking for trouble when I saw a Hun formation of about 60 machines–20 bombers and 40 fighters–at about 15,000 feet, and cursed the height we had lost. The fighters, mostly Messerschmitts, heeled over and came screaming down at us, and the next second we were in the thick of it. That attack developed like most dogfights into individual scraps. It was at about 10,000 feet that I found myself on the tail of my first Hun, a Messerschmitt 110. Most of my instruments, I remember, had gone haywire in the course of the violent manœuvring. I remember particularly that my giro was spinning crazily, and the artificial horizon had vanished somewhere into the interior of the instrument panel, calmly turning up its bottom and showing me the maker's stamp and the words Air Ministry Mark IV, or something like that.

Down went the Messerschmitt again with me close on his tail. With the great speed of the dive my controls were freezing solid, and I was fighting the stick hard to bring the Hun up into the centre of my sights. When you get them there they stick, in fact it's hard to get them out. Once there you can hold them for ever. I thumbed the trigger button just once, twice. I smelt the cordite fumes blowing back from my Brownings as the 1,200 squirts a minute from each of them went into him. I saw the little spurts of flame as the tracers struck. For a fraction of a second I saw the back outline of the pilot's head half-slewed around to see what was after him, before presumably he ceased to know. I saw a burst of flame and smoke from his engine, and then he was going down in a twirling spin of black smoke.

I looked around for the rest, but they were gone. My

own scrap had brought me about 30 miles inland, so I turned and headed back, noticing with a shock that my petrol reserve was just enough to get me home, provided that I ran into no more trouble. Dogfighting uses up juice at an enormous rate. About that first night–when you're going into it you think 'what fun', and when it's over you think 'how bloody dangerous'. Out over the North Sea and on the way back to the station I clicked on the radio and called up the pilots of my squadron one by one: 'How are you? Did you get any?' The first one came back jubilantly–he had got one. Then the rest–all of them had got one or two. One was funny. When I asked him what he had got, he came back, growling and disgusted, with a 'Graf Zeppelin'. Two didn't answer.

Back at the station we refuelled, reloaded, and were off again in a quarter of an hour. Back over Dunkirk at 10,000 feet we ran into a whole flock of Messerschmitts, which came charging down out of the clouds. They had obviously been sitting upstairs guarding some bombers hidden in the smoke below. They nearly caught us. I saw tracers going past my ears, and actually heard the gun rattle from one on my tail, and then he was gone. I followed him down, banging the throttle open and leaning on my stick, but in the last smoke clouds hanging over Dunkirk I lost him.

Up again, I saw the rest of the squadron at about 6,000. They were in a hell of a mix-up with the Hun fighters and some Junkers 88s, and I climbed up to join them. My radio was open, and as I climbed I could hear a stream of occasionally comic backchat passing backwards and for- wards between some of the other members of the squadron, occasionally punctuated with bursts of gunfire as they were popping off at Huns. Once, for instance, I heard a New Zealander calling and saying calmly, 'There's a Messerschmitt on your tail,' and the reply, 'Okay, pal,' and then I was in it too.

I picked out a Junkers 88 whose tail gunner got on to

me as soon as I engaged. The tracers of his guns sheered past me, seeming to curve lazily past my clear-vision window. You watch them quite calmly. They never look as though they were going to hit you, even when they are practically dead on. Again there was that lovely feeling of the gluey controls and the target being slowly hauled into the sights. Then thumb down on the trigger again and the smooth shuddering of the machine as the eight-gun blast let go. This time the squirt I gave him must have cut him in two. His tail folded back on his wings and there was a great smoke and flash of flame as he went down. As I spiralled down slowly after him, keeping a lookout for more, I saw one man bail out and his chute open.

The sky was nearly clear of Huns, and I turned round for home again, calling up the squadron as I went. This time we were all there, but our total bag was better than the first show. We had got 11 in all, making 19 in one morning for our two.

The second day we had a defined objective, but I detached two pilots to do some free-lance patrolling, one above the clouds which were at about 12,000 feet over Dunkirk and the other about 2,000 feet below. The rest of us went off toward Calais. About halfway there I heard the one above the clouds calling to the other in a deliberately affected sort of actor's voice, 'O, look what's coming, dearie, hordes and hordes of Messerschmitts. Nasty Messerschmitts.' And the answer back, 'Okay, pal, keep them busy. I'm coming upstairs.'

We swung round and started back. Making the quick turn out to sea I saw some Junkers guarded by Messerschmitts bombing a torpedo boat and some small rescue craft packed with troops far below. Chancing the anti-aircraft fire from the torpedo boat we plunged in. The Huns never saw us coming. Every one of us got one in that first dive. Stick back and screaming up again, we reformed, and then down once more. This time the Huns had scattered and it wasn't so easy. I got on to one

Messerschmitt who was scramming for home and got a squirt in. There was the usual burst of smoke from his engine as he went down. I followed, and I'm glad I did. Biding my time, I let him have it.

I didn't know then how they had got on with the Messerschmitt swarm they had got into above Dunkirk, but on the way back the first to answer my radio call said that he had got four. Then he suddenly said, 'Oh, hell, my engine's packed up.' Then, 'I'm on fire.' There was a silence for a second or two, and he said, 'Yippee! There's a destroyer downstairs. I'm bailing out.' A second later I heard him mutter, 'But how?'

It is, as a matter of fact, not easy to bail out of a Spitfire. The best way is to turn her over on her back and drop out through the hood–if you can. That, we found out, later, was exactly what he had done. He turned up in the mess three days afterwards wearing a naval sub-lieutenant's jacket and bell-bottom trousers, and carrying a sailor's kitbag over his shoulder.

That day for all its excitement was a poorer bag than we had expected–a total of 11. The third day we had the biggest show of all because then the evacuation was in full swing, and the Hun was throwing in everything he had in the way of aircraft to smash up the proceedings. We were now starting off at dawn, and on that day we went over Dunkirk and back again twice before breakfast-time, and my squadron was in 30 different combats.

On the second occasion my squadron ran into the biggest cloud of fighters that I'd seen so far. They were all Messerschmitt 109s, and there must have been pretty nearly one hundred of them. They seemed like a swarm of bees. We went in, however, and tore off a chunk each. My recollections of that show are a bit hazy because we were fighting upstairs and downstairs between 1,000 and 15,000 feet, and I was blacking-out fairly often in the pull outs after diving after a Hun. But I'm certain I got four, and the rest of the squadron wasn't doing too badly because at one time the air seemed to be full of burning aircraft. They were enemy planes all right, because we lost only one machine in that mad half-hour. The pilot of that one had his ailerons blown away, but managed to land on Dunkirk beach. He had a big gash in his forehead but managed to radio operations room at our station that he had 'landed safely'. He got on to Dunkirk jetty that night and came home with some of the BEF, getting back in mess that afternoon.

After finishing this first scrap with the 109s we ran into another bunch of 110s. We certainly got three Messerschmitts. They can dive very fast indeed. On that afternoon I remember following a Messerschmitt down from 15,000 and my needle had gone twice round the clock and off altogether before I decided to pull out. I must have been doing nearly 550 mph when I pulled out, but the Hun was still going. I think he went altogether into the ditch. All I remember is that I could not get the stick back, but had to use the tail-adjusting gear to pull out.

Instantly I felt the familiar blackout symptoms come on again, first the light turning yellow, then red, then slow darkness. You seem to be conscious, but you can't see nor, I think, hear because when you come out there is a sudden roar much louder than the ordinary sound of the motor.

That blooding we got over Dunkirk was instructive to all of us. Personally, I don't think that most of the Hun pilots are very good. I have come across a few who seem to enjoy fighting, but the bulk of them don't. They simply don't know their stuff. And our aircraft are certainly better.

They have got the numbers all right–or had–but I am more than ever sure that, however outnumbered you may be in dogfights at high speed, it boils down at any given moment to man against man.

The Spitfires Show Up

'Gun Buster' was the pseudonym of a writer who spent the early months of the war with the British military forces in France. He saw at first hand the bravery of the Spitfire pilots who helped rescue him and the other soldiers at Dunkirk, and here graphically recalls the event from his vantage point on the ground . . .

'We're due for a bit of excitement,' said the ACPO that afternoon.

'Haven't we had any yet?' I laughed.

'A hundred Spitfires are going to fly over us,' he continued.

'What?' I yelled, incredulous.

Remarkable as it may sound, Y-Battery, during all its wanderings from Brussels down to Arras and back to where we now were, had not been vouchsafed a single glimpse of an air fight. We had seen Germans brought down by our ack-ack fire, but never by any Allied planes. So far as we were concerned the sky was theirs, and we had to make the best of it.

I recalled that drop of bitter humour squeezed from one of our gunners at Givenchy under pressure of savage dive-bombing:

'And to think I once paid a shilling to see the Hendon Air Pageant!'

That summed it all up. Hence my incredulity on this occasion.

'A fact,' insisted the ACPO. 'We've just had it from RHQ.'

Shortly after, a large German bomber formation flew over our positions. We prepared for the usual heavy rain. Suddenly the sky changed. Down from heaven dropped a squadron of Spitfires, and also a number of Messerschmitt fighters. Within the twinkling of an eye we became sightseers of a grand battle. Almost immediately the German formation was broken up. A Spitfire sent one bomber crashing to the ground, while the occupants baled out. Dogfights commenced all over the sky. The air resounded with the incessant rat-tat-tat of machine-guns. In a few moments seven German parachutes were floating slowly down at the same time. Five German planes crashed in flames. A Spitfire drew out of the battle, circling and losing height, black smoke pouring from its tail. The only British loss, so far as I could see.

Y-Battery gazed on the battle with an excitement growing hotter each second. It was their first glimpse of our fighters in action since leaving Ninove, three weeks before. And it was appreciated!

'Now you *are* here, show us what you can do!' yelled the gunners to the skies.

Cheer mounted upon cheer as the Spitfires cut the Germans to ribbons.

'Another cokernut!' was the favourite cry whenever an enemy plane crashed.

It was all over in a quarter of an hour. But what a quarter! Like a revelation of a better world for us, after the long succession of days of unrelieved persecution from above. Yes, the most heartening quarter of an hour in Y-Battery's calendar for ages.

And for the time being the sky was ours. Marvellous . . .

The ACPO was jubilant. It might have been his own show.

47

'Does your old friend ever lead you astray?' he demanded proudly, as we retraced our footsteps to the Command Post. 'Didn't I prophesy we'd go back to England? Didn't I say the Spitfires were coming?'

'I don't think much of that as a bit of crystal-gazing,' I demurred. 'All you did was to take a message over the phone from RHQ. I could have done as much myself. But I won't appear niggardly. What's the next surprise in store for us?'

'Oh, nothing more today. Nothing more today,' he replied airily.

Let this be a warning to soothsayers that it is just as risky to forecast nothing as something . . .

The Spitfire Fund

In order to raise money to increase the number of Spitfires being built in the summer of 1940, Lord Beaverbrook, the Minister of Aircraft Production, had the ingenious idea of making a special appeal to the public. 'Please give us anything you can spare–however small–so that we can increase the numbers of this most potent fighter plane,' he urged. The response was almost unbelievable: in poured a cascade of money, from the sixpences of children and old age pensioners, to sums of four and five figures from wealthier citizens, companies of all sizes and even foreign countries. As a result of this, a good many Spitfires later took to the skies bearing the names of their donors–such as 'The Old Lady' (from Threadneedle Street), 'The Flying Scotsman' (Railwaymen), 'On The Target' (Army gunners), 'The Metal Trade' (from Australia), 'The Canadian Policeman', 'Queen Salote' (of Tonga), 'The Kalahari' (Bechuanaland) and even 'The Dog Fighter', sponsored by members of the Kennel Club!

Perhaps even more enterprising was Lord Beaverbrook's appeal for items made of aluminium which could be melted down and turned into Spitfires. Again there was a huge response from the housewives of Britain who gave up their pots and pans in such quantities that veritable mountains of them appeared all over the country! This appeal was, however, rather resented by some scrap metal dealers, and Lord Beaverbrook felt compelled to write a letter to The Times in answer to these criticisms, which is reprinted here. This furore led to the *Daily Sketch* headlining a report, 'From the Frying Pan into the Fire', while the whole business provided ideal material for the cartoonists and poets of *Punch* busy keeping up Britain's spirits–as the examples on these pages so amusingly show!

ALUMINIUM FOR SPITFIRES

An Appeal to Women by Lord Beaverbrook

Give us your aluminium. We want it, and we want it now. New and old, of every type and description, and all of it.

We will turn your pots and pans into Spitfires and Hurricanes, Blenheims and Wellingtons. I ask, therefore, that every one who has pots and pans, kettles, vacuum cleaners, hat-pegs, coat-hangers, shoe-trees, bathroom fittings and household ornaments, cigarette boxes, or any other articles made wholly or in part of aluminium, should hand them over at once to the local headquarters of the Women's Voluntary Services.

There are branches of this organisation in every town and village of the country. But if you are in any doubt, if you have any difficulty in finding the local office of the WVS, please inquire at the nearest police station or town hall, where you will be supplied with the necessary information.

The need is instant. The call is urgent. Our expectations are high.

July 10, 1940

Letter from Lord Beaverbrook to the Editor, The Times, *Saturday, July 13, 1940*

Sir, I have read the criticism in your columns of the aluminium appeal. It is twofold: (1) That there are ample stocks of scrap aluminium in the heaps; (2) That we should take the pots and pans from the shops.

Now as to the first, we do not want this scrap aluminium. It consists for the most part of inferior quality material which cannot be used in the manufacture of

50

aircraft. We want rolled aluminium. That is why we appeal for pots and pans, which are made of the right quality. If owners of scrap sort out any rolled aluminium that may be in their heaps we shall, of course, be glad to have it.

We cannot take the pots and pans from the shops. The cost would be too great for the small results we would achieve. No aluminium has been issued for the manufacture of pots and pans since the war started, and so the stocks in the shops must be low. If we were to requisition these stocks, we should set a very big precedent. And we should be acting contrary to the spirit of the appeal to the people to make a voluntary sacrifice for the national cause.

Yours etc.

EVERYBODY'S DOING IT

We're all buying Spitfires
As fast as we can buy
Spitfires and Hurricanes,
For battles in the sky . . .
The girls whose names are this or that,
The folk who keep a dog or cat,
The darts club and the foxhound packs,
The chimney-sweeps and steeplejacks,
The men who work in mine or mill,
Who milk our cows, our fields who till,
The rich and poor, the great and small,
The towns and counties one and all–
    They're all buying Spitfires
    (Hurricanes and Spitfires)
    As fast as they can buy.

They're all buying Spitfires,
The people near and far,
Hurricanes and Spitfires

To help to win the war . . .
In Port of Spain and Singapore,
And Chequerbent and Cockey Moor,
In Burma, Bluff and Table Bay,
And tiny islands far away,
In Durban, Malta and Fiji,
From John O'Groats to Tasman Sea,
In all the ends of all the earth
They're writing cheques for all they're worth–
  And they're all buying Spitfires
  (Hurricanes and Spitfires)
  To help to win the war . . .

They're all buying fighters,
 And as soon as they have done
They'll all be buying bombers
 To go and bust the Hun . . .

C.F.S.

Punch, September 25, 1940

LONDON CHIMES

Spitfires and Blenheims,
Said the bells of St Clements,
Aren't built for five farthings
Said the bells of St Martin's.
Donations, I pray ye,
Said the bells of Old Bailey;
On account o' the Blitz,
Said the bells of Shoreditch.
Downhearted? Not we!
Said the bells of Stepney;
Lor' love yer, no, no–
Boomed the big bell of Bow!

November 13, 1940

MORE ABOUT AERIAL SCRAP

Welcome! my departed Hoover,
I admire your last manœuvre;
Up above the world so high,
Sweeping Heinkels from the sky!

October 16, 1940

THE COST OF A SPITFIRE

(At the time of 'The Spitfire Fund' the following price list of the major component parts of a Spitfire was issued by the Air Ministry in the summer of 1940. Please note these prices are in the old pounds, shillings and pence!)

	£	s	d
Engine	2,000	0	0
Fuselage	2,500	0	0
Wings	1,800	0	0
Undercarriage	800	0	0
Guns	800	0	0
Tail	500	0	0
Propeller	350	0	0
Petrol Tank (Top)	40	0	0
Petrol Tank (Bottom)	25	0	0
Oil Tank	25	0	0
Compass	5	0	0
Clock	2	10	0
Thermometer	1	1	0
Sparking Plug		8	0

To these items can be added a further £1,000 for a variety of small parts such as screws, cables, switches, sockets, gauges and paint.

Battle of Britain

An Outline Chronology

June 30– July 1, 1940	Inconsequential German sorties seeking targets of opportunity. Skirmishing; shipping and south coast ports attacked.
July 10	Attacks increased significantly.
Mid-July	Bad weather limits enemy activity, but some RAF squadrons rotated.
July 19	141 Squadron Defiants move to Biggin Hill.
July 22/23	First victory for radar-equipped fighter.
Last week in July	Better German planning with an emphasis on free chase sweeps.
First week in August	A lull.
August 8	In convoy Peewit 16–20 ships lost.
August 9 and 10	Poor weather limits activities.

August 11	Change in German tactics leads to co-ordinated attacks on south coast ports, coastal airfields and radar chain Home Stations.
August 12	Two small convoys attacked but main enemy effort is against all fighter airfields in southern England. This day Bf 109s were 'tied' to escort duties.
August 13	*Eagle Day (Adlertag)*. Confusion in German communications. 45 German aircraft lost, 24 damaged. 2 Spitfires, 12 Hurricanes lost.
August 14	Light attacks.
August 15	*Black Thursday*. Co-ordinated attacks from the south and from German-occupied Scandinavia.
August 16	Flt Lt John Nicolson of 249 Squadron awarded VC: the only VC ever won by a pilot of Fighter Command.
August 18	The last time Stukas were used in numbers.
August 24	Luftwaffe steps up attacks against inland fighter stations. Co-ordinated widespread free chases. By day, German bomber inadvertently drops bombs on the outskirts of London.
August 24/25	First unopposed night raid on London. Churchill orders 'retaliatory' raid on Berlin.

August 30–	
September 6	Heyday of the free chase. RAF losses equivalent to one whole squadron each day. The crisis. Attacks by up to a Gruppe (30) of Bf 109s. On at least six occasions formations of 100 Bf 109s were used.
September 7	Shift of objectives–London attacked by day by more than 1,000 planes on a 10-mile front. Crocodile tactics. At least 38 British aircraft lost or damaged. More than 50 German aircraft lost, many of which crash-landed in France. Goering dissects the Geschwader tactics and orders Bf 109s into close support of the bombers. No. 11 Group has lost control of the situation.*
September 8–15	Respite. Scattered, light attacks on RAF fighter bases. Fighter squadrons rotated. Three new radar stations become operational.
September 15	Goering's final effort on the grand scale. Luftwaffe loses 87 aircraft. Fighter Command loses 40 fighters. All 11 Group's aircraft committed; no reserves and all major airfields in the Group totally vulnerable. Start of night attacks against London.
September 17	Operation Sealion postponed by Hitler.

* Another estimate for this day gives the figures as 28 RAF losses against 41 Luftwaffe. This same source states that on September 15, the losses were 26 RAF planes and 60 German.

| During remainder of September | Attacks on centres of aircraft production. Highflying Bf 109s in fighter-bomber role on intruder missions. |
| September 27 | Last major daylight raid. |

The Spitfire Squadrons

Twenty Spitfire Squadrons were operational during the Battle of Britain, and at the peak period on August 30 exactly 372 Spitfire Mark Is and IIs were flying. These are the Squadrons which remain immortalised in the term 'The Few'.

NUMBER TEN GROUP
(Headquarters, Box, Wiltshire)

Pembrey Sector Station
No. 92 Squadron under Squadron Leader P. J. Sanders

St. Eval Sector Station (Coastal Command)
No. 234 Squadron under Squadron Leader J. S. O'Brien

Middle Wallop Sector Station
No. 609 Squadron under Squadron Leader Horace Darley
No. 152 Squadron under Squadron Leader Peter Devitt

NUMBER ELEVEN GROUP
(Headquarters, Uxbridge, Middlesex)

Hornchurch Sector Station
No. 54 Squadron under Squadron Leader James Leathart
No. 65 Squadron under Squadron Leader A. L. Holland

No. 74 Squadron under Squadron Leader Francis White
No. 266 Squadron under Squadron Leader R. L. Wilkinson

Biggin Hill Sector Station
No. 610 Squadron under Squadron Leader John Ellis

Kenley Sector Station
No. 64 Squadron under Squadron Leader Aeneas MacDonell

NUMBER TWELVE GROUP
(Headquarters, Nottingham)

Church Fenton Sector Station
No. 616 Squadron under Squadron Leader Marcus Robinson

Kirton-in-Lindsey Sector Station
No. 222 Squadron under Squadron Leader Johnnie Hill

Digby Sector Station
No. 611 Squadron under Squadron Leader James McComb

Coltishall Sector Station
No. 66 Squadron under Squadron Leader Rupert Leigh

Duxford Sector Station
No. 19 Squadron under Squadron Leader P. C. Pinkham

NUMBER THIRTEEN GROUP
(Headquarters, Newcastle upon Tyne, Northumberland)

Catterick Sector Station
No. 41 Squadron under Squadron Leader H. R. L. Hood

Usworth Sector Station
No. 72 Squadron under Squadron Leader A. R. Collins
No. 79 Squadron under Squadron Leader Hervey Hayworth

Dyce Sector Station (Coastal Command)
No. 603 Squadron under Squadron Leader George Denholm

Turnhouse Sector Station
No. 602 Squadron under Squadron Leader A. V. R. Johnstone

Fighter Tactics

Gavin Lyall, the former RAF Pilot Officer and now best-selling novelist and author of such standard works as *Freedom's Battle: The RAF in World War Two*, here explains how the tactics employed by Spitfire pilots in their battles with German fighter planes had become a highly specialised and cunning business.

The basic tactics of reasonably evenly-matched aircraft had first been discovered in the First World War. Due to Air Council decisions that such tactics were outdated in the days of 'high-speed' monoplanes and that, anyway, Germany had no bases close enough to send over fighter-escorted raids, the RAF had to re-learn these tactics the hard way in the summer of 1940.

The myth that had to be forgotten was the idea that fighter battles were clean, chivalrous, knightly combats. It was the one form of war in which the object was to catch your enemy unaware, from behind, and shoot him in the back. All other tactics stemmed from this. They were:

1. Go as high as you can. Higher than your opponent, you can refuse battle or accept it at the most favourable moment. And you can cash height into speed by diving, and then, if you miss, re-cash it into height again, leaving him behind.

2. 'Beware the Hun in the sun.' All fighters, no matter what design, have one blind spot: directly into the sun. Attack out of the sun and your enemy may not see you until too late.

3. When attacked, turn *into* your attacker. If he comes from rear left, turn hard left: it makes him steepen his turn, perhaps more than he can control. If you turn the other way, all he has to do is come out of his turn and you are in his gunsight.

4. When you are in the circle that inevitably comes from this turn, turn as hard as you can and stay turning. You may come up behind him; the moment you stop turning, he is behind you.

5. It takes exactly the same time for you to approach and shoot down the aeroplane ahead as it does for the one behind to approach and shoot down you. So keep looking behind–it may make you miss, but it may make him miss you. Ideally, you should never fight alone, without a colleague whose job is to cover your tail so that you can concentrate ahead. So if alone, go home–as if you have all the devils of hell on your tail. You probably have.

6. This summed up all the other rules–keeping high and up-sun, watching behind, staying in good company–but was the most difficult to keep because it nevertheless contradicted the basic belief that makes a fighter pilot: *I am unbeatable*. Yet keeping this rule marked the great fighter leader, the one who led and survived, from the one who was led and who died. It was very simple: if you aren't going to win, don't get into the fight.

Until well after the war, when airborne radar and guided missiles became standard day-fighter equipment, no fighter design or formation could do more than stretch the rules. For example: in the circling fight, both pilots were in trouble. However, a properly handled Spitfire could usually out-turn and catch up on a Messerschmitt–but a Messerschmitt could sometimes dive out of the circle safely because its diving speed was higher.

The Spitfire Summer

Wing Commander Ronald Adams of Number Eleven Group was at the very heart of the frenzied activity of the Battle of Britain, and at the end of the war in 1945 was able to reflect objectively and vividly on what life had been like in the RAF that summer.

When I was ordered to report to Hornchurch in 1939 and first entered the operations room I wondered how long it would take me to assimilate and understand all the details of this queer room.

After a few weeks I found myself transferred to the Controller's Chair with all the business of radio-telephony patter to learn, and how to guide our own pilots to make contact with the enemy: for instance, 'bandits' meant German aircraft; so many 'angels' meant so many thousand feet in height; and the electric phrase 'tally-ho' from the pilot meant that your directions to him had been successful, and he had sighted the enemy and was going to engage him.

The days of that 'phoney' war were interesting because we were learning a new job. We practised with our aircraft incessantly, and every now and then the enemy obligingly put in an appearance over the North Sea and more often than not was successfully engaged. The radio stations round our coast–those tall masts that puzzled people before the war– were able to pick up and identify the enemy. The information was passed to us and our plotters plotted it with arrows on a great table map below us. We could find out the position of our own fighters from their radio transmissions, and so a thrilling game of hide-and-seek developed, while we waited for the 'tally-ho'. Radar was in its infancy in those days, and the enemy certainly did not appreciate its possibilities; nor, thank goodness, did we in Ops fully appreciate its limitations, or we might have been more worried. The technicians knew, of course, but they did not split. For it was not all that accurate, and there were times when it could fail to give any information at all. If the enemy had known just how to outwit it, which he could have done quite simply, the Battle of Britain would have had to be fought in a very different way, with perhaps a different ending.

The Battle of Holland, and of Belgium, and of France, developed and things were pretty tough, but it was Dunkirk that made my spirits rise again. I cannot believe that the much-vaunted Luftwaffe did not put out its best efforts to prevent the evacuation from those Dunkirk beaches, and it was then that the fighter boys showed just what they could do to the Luftwaffe. For the handful of them that were available 'clawed the enemy out of the sky'. I know that the army wondered where the aircraft were. They could not be expected to realise that a few dozen fighters were engaging hundreds of the enemy out of sight over the sea. I thought then, 'If that's what the fighters can do there's a hope for us, if only we can get some more.'

Then came the astonishing lull during July that puzzled us. We all knew how limited our resources were, how few aircraft and trained pilots we had got ready for action, and we did not–and we could not–understand why the enemy did not come for us at once. There was about a six weeks' pause. We held our breath during it, and then early in August, 1940, the radar plots began to show the enemy assembling in the air behind Cape Gris Nez in France. There he was milling around as one formation after another joined up, and we went to our loudspeakers when our Group Headquarters gave the order telling the squadron to take off. 'Scramble' was the word we used: 'Scramble', we would say, and Spitfires would tear into the sky and go off on their course over Maidstone, climbing up to 20,000 feet, to meet the oncoming enemy. As he came, we would sit there on the ground and watch the plots and gather such information as we could from the Royal Observer Corps and from our liaison officers. We would pass information to the pilots, telling them all changes in the enemy's direction, how he was splitting up into different formations, what height he was flying at, and guiding our fighters to the most advantageous position up in the eye of the sun, ready to attack. The Battle of Britain is summarised for me in one snatch on the radio-telephone from a famous New Zealand fighter who is still alive. I heard his voice in my ear as he sighted the enemy: 'Christ Almighty, tally-ho, whole bloody hordes of them.' That will for ever be to me the Battle of Britain–'whole hordes of them.'

During the next six weeks, as so many of us watched the battle in our skies in the south-east corner of England, from just before dawn until after last light of those days of outstanding summer weather, the Spitfires flew and flew, and the air crackled, not only with the explosions, but with the voices of the controllers on the radio and the answers of the pilots, and the breathless messages they passed to one another.

When we came out of that strange bungalow-building so near the main hangars of the aerodrome, we would stroll around in the sunlight to the pilots' dispersal huts on the other side and see them stretched out on beds, or in wicker chairs fast asleep, with the Mae Wests slung loosely upon them, and their clumsy flying-boots on their feet. Every time the telephone bell rang in the dispersal hut, or every time a voice was heard booming on the loudspeaker, all the sleeping figures would wake up and listen, and if it was not an urgent call for them, they would fall back and be asleep in an instant. Generally, the radio was on at full blast. That did not disturb them. The roar of aircraft taking off and the clatter of vehicles passing by–those did not disturb them either. But a telephone bell had them alert and grabbing for their flying-helmets before it had stopped ringing. Often, they were pretty nearly out on their feet. For instance, after a long day's flying, one of our boys landed and the Spitfire trundled along the ground and came to rest–and nobody got out of it. The ground-crew rushed out and tried to help their pilot, but he was slumped in his cockpit. He was not wounded; he was just fast asleep. The ground-crews themselves, stripped to the waist, worked day and night re-arming and re-fuelling and repairing, because the stock of replacements kept going down and the margin was getting narrower and narrower as the days went by. Occasionally, some lone ferry-pilot would arrive with a replacement–a new or patched-up Spitfire–but that was only on rare occasions. In those days and at the beginning of September, 1940, although I did not know it at the time, we were actually down to a few days' replacements, and that was all between us and many grim possibilities.

I do not think the boys had any conscious idea of being heroic. We none of us had any real knowledge of how desperate things were, in fact, but we realised without needing facts that this would be the end if it could not be withstood. The boys' abounding high spirits were rather stilled by September: they were strained and silent, but never for one instant did they fail to leap for their aircraft like scalded cats the moment the 'Scramble' was given. But when a wing went up, instead of the normal 36 aircraft taking the air, we would be lucky if we could scrape up ten. Solidly and speedily the enemy poured across the Straits of Dover, and still that magic eye of the radar spotted him and still the tired pilots went up to shoot him down, while he bombed their landing-grounds beneath them. I remember getting the depleted squadrons off the ground to meet an oncoming raid–and they were all off except the last section of three, when the bombs fell. All three aircraft had opened their throttles to take off; the first was blown upside down and slid about two hundred yards on its cockpit; the second was blown in the air and both its wings fell off; the third was blown clean out of the aerodrome and into a nearby brook. In the middle of the smoke and confusion, a pitched battle raged in the middle of the aerodrome. The undamaged pilot of the second aircraft had run to the first one: he had managed to pull the pilot of it out and was trying to carry him. Eric was a little fellow; he had a great admiration for the big, husky pilot he was trying to save, but the husky pilot had no wish to be saved by Eric, and the protests he made ended in a furious battle. This raid drove operations room from its aerodrome to an emergency pitch some some four miles away, in a small unoccupied grocer's shop, where we almost sat on one another's laps to control! We were bombed there within a few days.

So the heat was turned on, and grew throughout August and the opening days of September, until the historic day of September 15. I was controller on duty that night when my group rang through to give the score–185 enemy aircraft destroyed, 14 pilots lost on our side. It was not the end of the Battle of Britain, but it was the beginning of the end. Less and less enemy bombers came, with more and more enemy fighters trying to protect them. And now, more ferry-pilots arrived with more aircraft and more pilots to fly them. Still we knew there was much ahead to endure, but we also knew what we had suspected at Dunkirk had come true. We had taken the measure of the Luftwaffe and thrashed his hordes with a handful of fighter pilots, perhaps as many people as you would see collected round the field at a village cricket match.

An Eyewitness to Conflict

Charles Gardner, a BBC reporter, made broadcasting history on Sunday, July 14, 1940, when he gave an eyewitness account from the cliffs of Dover of an air battle taking place over the Channel. His excited description caused a sensation when it was aired, and though many people were thrilled by it, there were others who complained that it was 'not a proper subject for ring-side description'. Here is a transcript of that remarkable report, in which, of course, Spitfires are very much to the fore . . .

'The Germans are dive-bombing a convoy out at sea; there are one, two, three, four, five, six, seven German dive-bombers, Junkers 87s. There's one going down on its target now–Bomb! No! he missed the ships, it hasn't hit a single ship–there are about ten ships in the convoy, but he hasn't hit a single one and– There, you can hear our anti-aircraft going at them now. There are one, two, three, four, five, six–there are about ten German machines dive-bombing the British convoy, which is just out to sea in the Channel.

'I can't see anything. No! We thought he had got a German one at the top then, but now the British fighters are coming up. Here they come. The Germans are coming in an absolute steep dive, and you can see their bombs actually leave the machines and come into the water. You can hear our guns going like anything now. I am looking round now. I can hear machine-gun fire, but I can't see our Spitfires. They must be somewhere there. Oh! Here's one coming down.

'There's one going down in flames. Somebody's hit a German and he's coming down with a long streak—coming down completely out of control—a long streak of smoke—and now a man's baled out by parachute. The pilot's baled out by parachute. He's a Junkers 87, and he's going slap into the sea—and there he goes. *Smash!* A terrific column of water and there was a Junkers 87. Only one man got out by parachute, so presumably there was only a crew of one in it.

'Now, then, oh, there's a terrific mix-up over the Channel! It's impossible to tell which are our machines and which are Germans. There was one definitely down in this battle and there's a fight going on. There's a fight going on, and you can hear the little rattles of machine-gun bullets. Crump! That was a bomb, as you may imagine. Here comes one Spitfire. There's a little burst. There's another bomb dropping. Yes. It has dropped. It has missed the convoy. You know, they haven't hit the convoy in all this. The sky is absolutely patterned with bursts of anti-aircraft fire, and the sea is covered with smoke where the bombs have burst, but as far as I can see there is not one single ship hit, and there is definitely one German machine down. And I am looking across the sea now. I can see a little white dot of parachute as the German pilot is floating down towards the spot where his machine crashed with such a big fountain of water about two minutes ago.

'Well, now, everything is peaceful again for the moment. The Germans, who came over in about 20 or 25 dive-bombers, delivered their attack on the convoy, and I think they made off as quickly as they came. Oh yes, I can see one, two, three, four, five, six, seven, eight, nine, ten Germans hareing back towards France now for all they can go–and here are our Spitfires coming after them. There's going to be a big fight, I think, out there, but it will be too far away for us to see. Of course, there are a lot more German machines up there. Yes, there are one, two, three, four, five, six, seven on the top layer, one, two, three–there's two layers of German machines. They are all, I think, I could not swear to it, but they were all Junkers 87s.

'You can hear the anti-aircraft bursts still going.

'Well, that was a really hot little engagement while it lasted. No damage done, except to the Germans, who lost one machine and the German pilot, who is still on the end of his parachute, though appreciably nearer the sea than he was. I can see no boat going out to pick him up, so he'll probably have a long swim ashore.

'Well, that was a very unsuccessful attack on the convoy, I must say.

'Oh, there's another fight going on, away up, now–I think about 20, 25, or even 30,000 feet above our heads, and I can't see a thing of it. The anti-aircraft guns have put up one, two, three, four, five, six bursts, but I can't see the aeroplanes. There we go again– Oh, we have just hit a Messerschmitt. Oh, that was beautiful! He's coming right down. I think it was definitely that burst got him. Yes, he's come down. You hear those crowds? He's finished! Oh, he's coming down like a rocket now. An absolutely steep dive. Let us move round so we can watch him a bit more. Here he comes, down in a steep dive–the Messerschmitt. No, no, the pilot's not getting out of *that* one. He's being followed down. What, there are two more Messerschmitts up there? I think they are all right. No– that man's finished. He's going down from about 10,000, oh, 20,000 to about 2,000 feet, and he's going straight down–he's not stopping. I think that's another German machine that's definitely put paid to. I don't think we shall actually see him crash, because he's going into a bank of cloud. He's smoking now. I can see smoke, although we cannot count that a definite victory because I did not see him crash. He's gone behind a hill. He looked certainly out of control.

'Now we are looking up to the anti-aircraft guns. There's another! There's another Messerschmitt. I don't know whether he's down or whether he's trying to get out of the anti-aircraft fire, which is giving him a very hot time. There's a Spitfire! Oh, there's about four fighters up there, and I don't know what they are doing. One, two, three, four, five fighters fighting right over our heads. Now there's one coming right down on the tail of what I think is a Messerschmitt, and I think it's a Spitfire behind him. Oh, darn! They've turned away and I can't see. I can't see. Where's one crashing? No, I think he's pulled out. You can't watch these fights very coherently for long. You just see about four twirling machines, you just hear little bursts of machine-gunning, and by the time you've picked up the machines they've gone. Hullo, there are one, two, three; and look, there's a dogfight going on up there—there are four, five, six machines wheeling and turning around. Now—hark at the machine guns going! Hark! one, two, three, four, five, six; now there's something coming right down on the tail of another. Here they come; yes, they are being chased home—and *how* they are being chased home! There are three Spitfires chasing three Messerschmitts now. Oh, boy! Look at them going! Oh, look how the Messerschmitts!—Oh, boy! that was really grand! There's a Spitfire behind the first two. He will get them. Oh yes, Oh, boy! I've never seen anything so good as this. The RAF fighters have really got these boys taped. Our machine is catching up the Messerschmitt now. He's catching it up! He's got the legs of it, you know. Now right in the sights. Go on, George! You've got him! Bomb—bomb. No, no, the distance is a bit deceptive from here. You can't tell, but I think something definitely is going to happen to that first Messerschmitt. Oh yes—just a moment—I think I wouldn't

71

like to be in that first Messerschmitt. I think he's got him. Yes? Machine-guns are going like anything. No, there's another fight going on. No, they've chased him right out to sea. I can't see, but I think the odds would be certainly on that first Messerschmitt catching it. Where? I can't see them at all. Just on the left of those black shots. See it? Oh, yes, oh yes, I see it. Yes, they've got him down, too. I can't see. Yes, he's pulled away from him. Yes, I think that first Messerschmitt has been crashed on the coast of France all right.'

Air Strike

Group Captain Sir Douglas Bader, the 'tin legs' hero and one of the most famous fighter pilots of World War Two, commanded a Spitfire wing at Tangmere in 1941. Of the many stories of his skill and bravery which are told, the following report, given by himself, is the one which I find the most engrossing–perhaps because the fight in question just happened to take place over the town of Enfield in Middlesex where I was a small child at that very same time . . .

Thirteen of our squadron were on patrol near London looking for the Germans, who we knew were about in large formations. Soon we spotted one large formation, and it was rather an awe-inspiring sight–particularly to anyone who hadn't previously been in action. I counted 14 blocks of six aircraft–all bombers–with 30 Messerschmitt 110 fighters behind and above, so that altogether there were more than 100 enemy aircraft to deal with.

Four of the boys had gone off to check up on some unidentified aircraft which had appeared shortly before we sighted the big formation, and they weren't back in time to join in the fun. That left nine of us to tackle the big enemy formation.

I detailed the pilot to my right to take his section of three Spitfires up to keep the 30 Messerschmitts busy. 'OK, OK,' he said, with obvious relish, and away he streaked to deal with that vastly superior number of enemy fighters.

The remaining six of us tackled the bombers. They were flying at 15,000 feet with the middle of the formation roughly over Enfield, heading east. When we first sighted them they looked just like a vast swarm of bees.

With the sun at our backs and the advantage of greater height, conditions were ideal for a surprise attack, and as soon as we were all in position, we went straight down on them. We didn't adopt any set rule in attacking them–we just worked on the axiom that the shortest distance between two points is a straight line.

I led the attack and went for what I think was the third block of six from the back. And *did* those Huns break up! In a few seconds there was utter confusion. They broke up all over the sky!

As I went through, the section I aimed at fanned out. I can't give an exact sequence of events, but I know that the pilot who followed immediately behind took the one that broke away to the right. The third man in our line went straight through and gave the rear gunner of a Hun in one of the middle blocks an awful shock. Then the other boys followed on, and things really began to get moving.

Now, there's one curious thing about this air fighting. One minute you see hundreds of aeroplanes in the sky, and the next minute there's nothing. All you can do is to look through your sights at your particular target–and look in your mirror, too, if you are sensible, for any Messerschmitts that might be trying to get on to your tail.

Well, that particular battle lasted five or ten minutes, and then, quite suddenly, the sky was clear of aircraft.

One pilot had sent a Hun bomber crashing into a greenhouse. Another bomber had gone headlong into a field filled with derelict motor cars–it hit one of the cars, turned over, and caught fire. Another of our chaps had seen a twin-engined job of sorts go into a reservoir near

Enfield. Yet another pilot saw his victim go down with his engine flat out–the plane dived into a field and disintegrated into little pieces. Incidentally, that particular pilot brought down three Huns that day.

We hadn't shot the entire formation down, of course. The bombers hadn't waited for that, but all made off home in all directions at high speed. But, apart from our bag of 12 (eight Messerschmitt 110 fighter-bombers, three Heinkel 111 bombers, and a fourth Heinkel bomber already partly damaged by another squadron), there were a number of others which were badly shot up and probably never got home–like one which went staggering over Southend with one engine out of action.

As there was nothing else left to shoot at we went home, picking up as we went the infuriated section which had been sent off to investigate the unidentified aircraft and had missed our battle. They hadn't fired a single round between the four of them–and their language when they heard what they'd missed was unprintable!

Shot Down by My Own Side!

Group Captain Brian Kingcome was another of the great Spitfire aces and served with No. 92 Squadron. He was officially credited with 11 'kills', but his total was probably nearer 20. Here he reminisces on the Battle of Britain and another personal and rather less auspicious incident . . .

I suppose killing takes many forms. When you kill people in the RAF it's a very detached sort of feeling. You're not shooting at a person so much as an aeroplane.

Different people have different temperaments, of course. Some people liked killing long before they went into the war. They didn't just get into the habit then.

For me it was always a case of mixed emotions when personalities came into it–when you're shooting an aeroplane down and you suddenly realise there's a chap in there. Mostly it's totally impersonal. But I think it was always pleasing to see the other pilot get out of his plane.

It seemed to me that you weren't doing what you were meant to do if you went up and picked on one or two planes and shot them down, and then followed them down to confirm victories.

The main object was to stop a large bomber formation from reaching its target. The only way to do that was to leap into the middle of them and run amok, firing at everything in sight, hitting as many as you could, as often as you could. It's extraordinary how this demoralised the Germans–you could turn a whole wave of bombers by that sort of action.

If you just nipped round the edges and picked off one here and there and followed them down, it took you out of the battle.

When I was flying from Biggin Hill with 92 Squadron, we'd try to tackle the bombers head-on rather than from the flank, because it was bloody frightening for the poor chap flying the enemy plane. If you've ever sat at the front of one of those German bombers you'll know you're utterly vulnerable–nothing in front of you except glass. If you suddenly see planes coming at you from the front, you get a bit jumpy!

Also, it was safer for us. The bombers could bring far fewer guns to bear on us that way. And the main thing was to upset the pilot rather than shoot the rear gunner.

In battle, there seems to be an unwritten rule that when you're fighting over your own territory there's a bit more emotion attached–an Englishman's home being his castle, and all that. It sounds corny, but it's true. I mean you see a wave of bombers approaching your favourite pub and you start taking a bit of action!

Over the years the story of the Battle of Britain has been tremendously exaggerated. I'm not trying to play it down, but I think it has been overplayed in relation to a whole lot of equally formidable campaigns.

I mean, for a start, we had the chance of flying a Spitfire, which was a marvellous plane. The Battle of Britain was actually a very comfortable war. You lived in a nice, comfortable mess, though admittedly you took off rather early in the morning sometimes; you got better food than most people; and you went back to a warm bed at night. The creature comforts were provided for.

When you compare that, for instance, to the Russian convoys, or the Battle of the Atlantic, which I think was a ghastly, bloody war–those chaps sitting on tankers for weeks and maybe getting drowned at the end of it–well, a Spitfire flight only took about an hour and a quarter.

Can you imagine being on a tanker going to and fro across the Atlantic, which took about a fortnight, with those bloody periscopes coming up out of the water? In a convoy you were just a target. There *was* the hope of getting through–but you were absolutely helpless.

Now, in the air you were pretty highly-trained chaps, and we had first-class equipment, so we could do something if attack came. Also, I think one knows it can 'never happen to me'. That sustains everybody.

Mind you, it did *once* happen to me! I was shot down at the end of a battle–and by a Spitfire!

This actually happened quite often–a Spitfire shooting down a Spitfire. With inexperienced chaps and the sky full of planes, there wasn't all that much difference between our fighters and theirs at certain angles. We camouflaged the planes at first, trying to make the wretched things invisible, but then our own anti-aircraft guns used to go for us, so we gave them a more spectacular underside.

The incident in question happened over Maidstone on October 15, 1940. There had been an engagement, and I was gliding back to Biggin Hill after using up all my ammunition. I remember it was a beautiful day and I could see Biggin Hill in the distance.

I throttled back at about 25,000 feet. There was nothing in the sky except three Spitfires behind me.

Then, suddenly–bang! The aeroplane was full of holes. I was bloody indignant I can tell you.

All at once I realised, 'Christ! I've got to bail out!' I had a bullet through one leg and my controls had gone. I *had* to get out!

As I was parachuting down I remembered that I was wearing a German Mae West! It was one that had been taken from a crashed plane–they were a sight more comfortable than ours. At that I began to get very worried.

There I was, dangling on my parachute going down outside Maidstone, and I could see a crowd gathering below. What if someone decided to take a shot at me, I thought!

I believe there were instructions then to the Home Guard on how to deal with parachutists–apparently some of the Germans were coming down disguised as nuns! So one instruction said, 'In order to ascertain sex of parachutist, put hand up skirt.' Those were certainly desperate times!

Anyhow, I landed safely, and the crowd soon realised from my language that I was English.

In fact, as I said, it was by no means uncommon to be shot down by your own planes. I could name you half a dozen who were–the commander of Biggin Hill for one. And another chap I know of was *deliberately* shot down and killed by his own squadron. They didn't like him, apparently.

I can also tell you that some of our own chaps even shot the odd pilot in a parachute after they had shot down his plane. If you hit them with a shell you could knock them right round the parachute.

I know of more than one Pole who did that–but you could understand it in their case. Some of those Poles had seen their families slaughtered, and they had the most desperate, bitter hatred of the Germans.

But most of my memories of the Battle of Britain are of it being very exciting and a most enjoyable campaign. It was entirely up to your own initiative how you attacked. You had to use your own skill and judgement. That in itself was exciting.

I don't think anyone who was in it wouldn't willingly go through it all again if it were necessary. It was certainly the most satisfying campaign of the war.

A Bag of Five Jerries

Sergeant Pilot R. F. Hamlyn of No. 610 Squadron notched up perhaps the most remarkable achievement of the war when he shot down five Germans with his Spitfire on August 24, 1940. Here he relates that momentous day in a typically self-deprecating manner.

Saturday was certainly a grand day. It started with the dawn. We were up at a quarter past four. We were in the air just after five o'clock. Shortly before half past eight we were in the air again looking for enemy raiders approaching the south coast from France. We saw three or four waves of Junkers 88s, protected by a bunch of Messerschmitt 109s above. We were at 15,000 feet, between the bombers and the fighters. The fighters did not have much chance to interfere with us before we attacked the bombers.

I attacked one of the waves of bombers from behind and above. I selected the end bomber of the formation, which numbered between 15 and 18. A burst of fire lasting only two seconds was enough. It broke away from the formation, dived down, and I saw it crash into the sea.

I then throttled back so that I would not overtake the whole formation. I was getting quite a lot of cross-fire from the other bombers as it was, though none of it hit me. If I had broken away after shooting down the first

R.J. Mitchell, the creator of the Spitfire

The prototype Spitfire on its first flight in 1936

A cut-away sketch
of the Spitfire by
G.H. Davis
published during
the Battle of Britain

The Spitfire's
powerful Rolls
Royce Merlin
engine

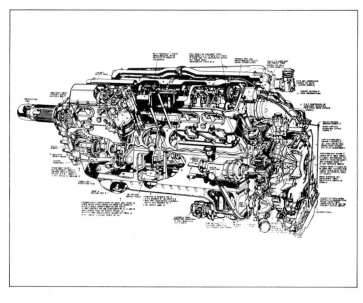

The cockpit of a Spitfire

TEN of MY RULES for AIR FIGHTING.

1 Wait until you see the whites of his eyes.
   Fire short bursts of 1 to 2 seconds and only when your sights are definitely 'ON'.

2 Whilst shooting think of nothing else, brace the whole of the body, have both hands on the stick, concentrate on your ring sight.

3 Always keep a sharp lookout. "Keep your finger out"!

4 Height gives You the initiative.

5 Always turn and face the attack.

6 Make your decisions promptly. It is better to act quickly even though your tactics are not the best.

7 Never fly straight and level for more than 30 seconds in the combat area.

8 When diving to attack always leave a proportion of your formation above to act as top guard.

9 INITIATIVE, AGGRESSION, AIR DISCIPLINE, and TEAM WORK are words that MEAN something in Air Fighting.

10 Go in quickly – Punch hard – Get out!

Spitfire pilot 'Sailor' Malan's rules for air fighting

A typical Battle of Britain cartoon from *Punch*

". . . I put my airplane into a screaming vertical dive, the eight guns of my Spitcane belching death to the Nazi invader!"

The Spitfire – and the men who flew her in the Battle of Britain: two
photographs from the American magazine, *Flying*

Just a few of the Spitfire's victims: a page of shot-down German aircraft
from the *Illustrated London News,* 24 August, 1940

One of several films to feature the Spitfire, *Malta Story*, which starred Alec Guinness and Anthony Steele (1953)

Filming a scene from the famous movie, *Battle of Britain*, with Robert Shaw in the cockpit of a Spitfire (1969)

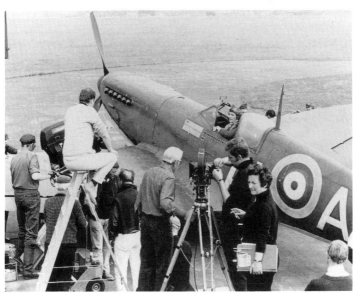

One of the war-time Spitfires which is still flying today

Keeping the legend alive – Steve Atkins, Spitfire restorer

bomber I should have exposed myself to the full force of the enemy formation's cross-fire. I didn't have time to select another bomber as target, for almost immediately a Messerschmitt 109 came diving after me. As I had throttled back he overshot me, and presented me with a beautiful target. He pulled up about 150 yards in front of me. I pressed the gun-button for two seconds. He immediately began to smoke, and dived away. I followed him and saw him go straight into the sea. When the sky was clear of German planes we went home for breakfast.

I didn't get any breakfast. I only had time for a hot drink before we were ordered to stand by again, and by half past eleven that morning we were patrolling the south-east coast. We were attacked by half a dozen Messerschmitt 109s, and, of course, we broke up to deal with them individually. I had a dogfight with one, both of us trying to get into position to deliver an attack on the other, but I outmanœuvred him. I got on his tail, and he made off for the French coast as hard as he could go.

The fight started at 10,000 feet. We raced across the Channel like mad. As we were going like that I saw one of our fellows shoot down another Messerschmitt, so I said to myself, 'I must keep the squadron's average up and get this one.' I didn't fire at him until we were actually over the French coast. Then I let him have it–three nice bursts of fire lasting three seconds each, which, as you may imagine, is an awfully long time!

I started the final burst at 8,000 feet, and then he began to go down, and I followed until I saw him crash into a field in France. Then I went back home without seeing any enemy at all. I carefully examined my Spitfire after I landed, certain that I must have been hit somewhere. But, no, not a mark. It was very satisfactory.

Our third show began just before four o'clock in the afternoon. We were flying towards the Thames Estuary at 5,000 feet when we saw anti-aircraft shells bursting in the sky to the north-east. We changed course and began to climb for the place where we thought we should meet the enemy. We did. They were flying at 12,000 feet. Twenty Junkers 88s in tight formation accompanied by about 20 Messerschmitt 109s above them. They were flying towards the London area. We could see the balloons shining in the sun. We pulled up towards the fighters. I got under one Messerschmitt and gave him two bursts.

Smoke started to pour out of him, and he went down out of control. Suddenly, tracer bullets started whizzing past my machine. I turned sharply, and saw a Messerschmitt attacking one of our pilots. I turned on the attacker and gave him a quick burst. Immediately he began to slow down and the aircraft began to smoke. I pressed the gun-button a second time, and the Messerschmitt caught fire.

I fired a third time, and the whole machine became enveloped in flames and pieces began to fly off. Finally, as it went down, more pieces came off, all burning. As it tumbled down towards the Thames Estuary it was really a bunch of blazing fragments instead of a whole aircraft. It was an amazing sight. That was my fifth for the day and the squadron's ninety-ninth. The squadron brought the score over the century the next day.

There is a lot of luck about air fighting. I mean it's a matter of luck whether you get into a good scrap or not. I was right through the Dunkirk show and didn't get a thing. But recently I seem to have been lucky. Fights are over so quickly that unless you are right there at the beginning you are liable not to see anything at all. None of the fights today lasted more than five minutes each.

Boy in a Spitfire

Quentin Reynolds, the famous American foreign correspondent who reported the entire war from the front line, had a particular interest in aerial warfare, as he reveals in this dispatch from an English aerodrome in 1940. Apart from narrating the film, *Eagle Squadron* (1942), about US pilots flying Spitfires, he also helped immortalise the plane in his books, *The Battle of Britain* (1953) and *They Fought For The Sky* (1958).

At one of the aerodromes near the Channel there was a squadron of 12 Spitfires. It was six in the morning, the kind of morning when it feels good to be alive. The pilots were in their tent listening to a portable radio, and the ground crew were playing soccer.

The squadron leader, quite young, had downed 18 German planes, and had ribbons on his chest. 'I want you to meet a new kid who joined us yesterday,' he said. 'Today will be his first show.'

The new pilot was Art Donahue of Laredo, Texas, one of the 30 Americans in the RAF. We hadn't spoken a dozen words when the telephone rang. The ground crew stopped kicking the ball around. The leader answered the phone. 'Twelve or more heading for convoy off Dover. Yes, sir.'

I looked at my watch. It was exactly 6.05. All the leader

said was, 'A scramble,' the RAF term for a fight.

The men climbed into their planes and put helmets on. They didn't look like kids any more. It was 6.09 as the last plane got off the ground. Flying in sections of three, they circled to gain height, went up to 10,000 feet, and headed for the convoy.

Down at the other end of the aerodrome 12 Hurricanes roared off to join the fight. They would be back soon, for fighters carry petrol for an hour and a half only. But time passed very slowly.

It was just seven when the Spitfires reappeared. I watched them. There was something uneven about the formation. Then I realized that one of them was missing.

They landed and taxied up to the tent. According to routine, the leader reported to an intelligence officer. Then each pilot gave his personal report. In that way a good idea of the damage to the enemy is obtained.

The leader said, 'We met halfway over the Channel, at 14,000 feet. There were 20 Heinkels and 21 109s and 110s. We came out of the sun and I sent a four-second burst at a Heinkel. It drove toward the sea, smoke pouring from it. A 110 got on my tail, and I banked into a cloud. Angling up another thousand, I ran into two Heinkels. I sent a three-second burst into one of them. He crashed into the sea. The other dived and I sent two bursts. He was badly hurt and I followed him all the way down. At 500 feet he burst into flames. There were no other enemy aircraft in sight. I collected the squadron and we came home.'

'Is that all?' the intelligence officer asked.

'Yes. Except Isaacs failed to return. He got separated from the squadron. I don't know how.'

'I saw him.' The pilot who spoke was a lad named Douglas—tall, slim, with a baby face. 'I saw him with two 110s on his tail. By the time I got to him he went down. He had no chance to bale out.'

One by one they told their stories. 'I make it seven

confirmed enemy casualties and four unconfirmed,' the intelligence officer said. For a plane to be listed officially as shot down the pilot must pledge his word of honour that he has seen it crash. When you see a story saying that 20 German planes were downed, the chances are that eight or nine others suffered the same fate.

Donahue, the American kid, looked at his Spitfire. There was a hole in the fuselage you could stick your fist through.

'You put up a great show,' the leader said to him. 'When did you get hit?'

'When I was on the tail of an Me 110,' he said ruefully. 'I felt a jar and then my controls went haywire. Even my sights were acting funny. I sent one burst at the Me, but didn't get him. But it was fun while it lasted.'

Donahue turned to me and grinned. 'Seven weeks ago I left Texas, went to Ontario, enlisted, and within three days was on a boat.'

'He had 1,800 hours,' the leader said. 'He needed only a week's training in order to handle a Spitfire.'

A lone Spitfire taxied up to the tent. A pilot climbed out and saluted the leader.

'I was told to report to you, sir.'

'Righto; meet the boys and have some tea.'

There was a silence for a moment. Every one was thinking of Isaacs. Now the squadron was a squadron again.

Young Douglas said to me rather shyly, 'Would you like to see how a Spitfire works?'

He was like a child showing off a new toy. When he explained things his face lighted.

I sat in the plane and handled the controls. The bullet-proof glass in the windshield is nearly three inches thick. At the top of the windshield there is a rear-view mirror.

'That's a big help,' Douglas grinned. 'The mirror tells us if a plane is on our tail.'

'What do you do then?'

Douglas laughed. 'Pray and get the hell away from him.'

The 'stick' on a Spitfire is a wheel about five inches across. There is a small button on the wheel. While flying you hold the wheel in your right hand, the throttle in your left. When you sight an enemy you get your back to the sun and peer through the sight, a heavy oblong glass with a red circle and crossing lines. When the enemy plane is covered by the crossed lines, you press the button with your thumb and eight guns bark. You can't see the guns, because they are flush with the wings.

'This wireless is wonderful,' Douglas said. 'This morning, we didn't sight the Jerries until we were about ten miles over the Channel. Then the squadron leader saw them and yelled to us, "Tallyho! Tallyho! There they are!"'

'I was after a Heinkel when one of the lads called to me, "You'd better look behind you!" I did, and saw an Me coming at me. I did a sharp vertical climb and got away. Then I saw the lad who'd warned me, and damned if there weren't two on his tail. I yelled back, "So had you!"'

'Did he look behind?' I asked.

'That was Isaacs,' he said simply.

It was a job for me to get out of the small cockpit. I asked Douglas how it was possible to bale out.

'Three days ago my ship was on fire,' he laughed. 'I couldn't get out of the darn' thing. Then I found a swell trick. I unfastened my belt, turned the plane on its back and just fell out. The Channel water is damned cold, too.'

'Who picked you up?'

'One of those little motor torpedo boats. The squadron leader had the nerve to tell me I baled out just to get a new uniform.'

We went back into the tent. It was almost ten. At ten this squadron would be through. Then they'd fly inland for an eight-hour rest.

But at fifteen minutes to ten the phone rang. The squadron leader said, 'Yes, yes; that's all right; we don't mind. Twelve off Folkestone. Righto.'

The motors roared into action. I gave Douglas a boost into the cockpit.

'Good luck, kid,' I shouted.

'I might need it,' he yelled back, grinning.

He needed more luck than I had to give him. *Fifteen minutes later the boy was dead.*

'Achtung, Spitfeuer!'

General Major Adolf Galland was the most decorated German fighter ace of the war–a man hero-worshipped by his own pilots and admired by opposing British airmen for his skill, bravery and sense of chivalry. Galland himself had a real respect for the Spitfire, as he confesses in these memories of the conflict.

The second phase of the Battle of Britain, lasting from July 24 to August 8, 1940, was essentially a fighter battle. On its opening day I was with my wing for the first time in action over England. Over the Thames Estuary we got involved in a heavy scrap with Spitfires, which were screening a convoy. Together with the Staff Flight, I selected one formation as our prey, and we made a surprise attack from a favourably higher altitude. I glued myself to the tail of the plane flying outside on the left flank and when, during a righthanded turn, I managed to get in a long burst, the Spitfire went down almost vertically. I followed it until the cockpit cover came flying towards me and the pilot baled out, then followed him down until he crashed into the water. His parachute had failed to open.

The modern Vickers Supermarine Spitfires were slower than our planes by about 10 to 15 mph, but could perform steeper and tighter turns. The older Hawker Hurricane, which was at that time still frequently used by the British, compared badly with our Me 109 as regards speed and rate of climb. Our armament and ammunition were also undoubtedly better. Another advantage was that our engines had injection pumps instead of the carburettors used by the British, and therefore did not conk out through lack of acceleration in critical moments during combat. The British fighters usually tried to shake off pursuit by a half-roll or half-roll on top of a loop, while we simply went straight for them, with wide-open throttle and eyes bulging out of their sockets.

During this first action we lost two aircraft. That was bad, although at the same time we had three confirmed kills. We were no longer in doubt that the RAF would prove a most formidable opponent.

*   *   *

It was in August that Reichsmarschall Göring came to visit us on the coast of France. The large-scale attacks of our bombers on Britain were imminent, and the air supremacy necessary for them had not been achieved to the degree expected. The British fighter force was wounded, it was true, but not beaten. And our pursuit Stuka and fighter force had naturally suffered grievous losses in material, personnel and morale. The uncertainty about the continuation of the air offensive reflected itself down to the last pilot. Göring refused to understand that his Luftwaffe, this shining and so far successful sword, threatened to turn blunt in his hand. He believed there was not enough fighting spirit and a lack of confidence in ultimate victory. By personally taking a hand, he hoped to get the best out of us.

To my mind, he went about it the wrong way. He had nothing but reproaches for the fighter force, and he expressed his dissatisfaction in the harshest terms. The theme of fighter protection was chewed over again and again. Göring clearly represented the point of view of the bombers and demanded close and rigid protection. The bomber, he said, was more important than record bag figures. I tried to point out that the Me 109 was superior in the attack and not so suitable for purely defensive purposes as the Spitfire, which, although a little slower, was much more manœuvrable. He rejected my objection. We received many more harsh words. Finally, as his time ran short, he grew more amiable and asked what were the requirements for our squadrons. Mölders asked for a series of Me 109s with more powerful engines. The request was granted. 'And you?' Göring turned to me. I did not hesitate long. 'I should like an outfit of Spitfires for my group.' After blurting this out, I had rather a shock, for it was not really meant that way. Of course, fundamentally I preferred our Me 109 to the Spitfire, but I was unbelievably vexed at the lack of understanding and the stubbornness with which the command gave us orders we could not execute–or only incompletely–as a result of many shortcomings for which we were not to blame. Such brazen-faced impudence made even Göring speechless. He stamped off, growling as he went.

* * *

Almost a year after this I had an encounter with Spitfires which I shall never forget. The day was June 21, a sunny, summer day. About noon the radar station reported, 'Large formation of enemy aircraft approaching'. As we found out later, it was a force of Bristol Blenheim bombers with a fighter escort of about 50 Spitfires and Hurricanes. They were raiding St. Omer, a favourite target of the British in those days. I gave the alarm and sent up all three wings. They soon engaged the enemy in a battle which cost both sides heavy losses.

At 12.24 I took off with the squadron detailed as the leading unit of the group, and at an altitude of 10,000 feet we sighted the British formations which had just raided the airfield of Arques, near St. Omer. From a greater height I dived right through the fighter escort on to the main bomber force and attacked the right plane of the lower rear row from very close. The Blenheim caught fire immediately. Some of the crew baled out and the plane exploded on crashing near the airfield of St. Omer. The time was 12.32, eight minutes after take-off. Kill No. 68.

In the meantime, my unit was wrestling with Spitfires and Hurricanes. My section companion and I were the only Germans at the moment attacking the bombers, and I immediately started my second attack. Again I managed to dive through the fighters. This time it was a Blenheim in the leading row of the formation. Flames and black smoke poured from her starboard engine, she broke away from the formation, and I saw two parachutes open. The time was 12.36. Kill No. 69.

Then Spitfires were on my tail. Tracer bullets whizzed past me. I tried to shake them off with a sharp downward bank, and got rid of my pursuer, but I had caught a packet and a layer of haze enveloped me, my right radiator was shot up, and I was leaving a long trail of smoke behind. A little later the engine seized up. Emergency landing! Luckily, I was able to make a harmless crash-landing on the airfield of Calais-Marck, just below me. Half an hour later an Me 108 collected me and brought me back to my group.

After lunch the dance continued. At four o'clock there was a new alarm, 'Strong British fighter formations approaching from the Channel,' and all airworthy machines were up again and at the enemy. My faithful section companion, Rottenflieger Hegenauer, who had flown almost all the sorties against England with me during the previous year, had been shot down almost at the same time as myself, so I started alone. South-east of Boulogne I sighted my No. 1 Wing, and decided to join them. Slightly lower and to port of them was a Spitfire formation. I immediately attacked one of the last planes of the formation–unfortunately, not *the* last, but the Spitfire I went after crashed in flames. Kill No. 70. A nice even number, I thought, as I followed her down to register the kill. I had no witness, as I was flying alone.

Hell broke loose in my crate. Now they've got you! That's what happens if you take your eye off for a couple of seconds! Something hard hit my head and arm. My aircraft was in bad shape, the wings ripped by cannon fire, and I myself was sitting half in the open. The right side of the fuselage had been shot away and fuel tank and radiator were both leaking heavily. Instinctively, I banked away to the north, noticing almost calmly as I did so that my heavily damaged plane still flew and responded tolerably well with the engine cut off. My luck has held once more, I was thinking, and I will try to glide home. My altitude was 18,000 feet.

My arm and head were bleeding, but I didn't feel any pain. No time for that. Anyhow, nothing precious was hurt. A sharp detonation tore me out of my reverie–the tank, which up to then had been gurgling away quietly, suddenly exploded and the whole fuselage was immediately aflame. Burning petrol ran into the cockpit. I was getting uncomfortably hot. Only one thought remained: Get out! Get out! The cockpit roof-release–would not work–must be jammed. Shall I burn alive in here? I tore my belt open, tried to open the hinged top of the roof, but the air pressure on it was too strong. There were flames all around me. You must open it! You must not fry to death in here! Terror. Those were the most fearful seconds of my life. With a last effort I pushed my whole body against the roof. The flap opened and was torn away by the air-stream. I had already pulled her nose up but the push against the joystick did not throw me entirely clear of the burning coffin which a few minutes before was still my faithful Me 109. The parachute on which I had been sitting was caught on the fixed part of the cockpit roof. The entire plane was now in flames and was dashing down to earth with me. With my arm around the aerial mast, I tugged and pushed against anything I could find with my feet–all in vain! Should I be doomed at the last moment, although I was already half-freed? I don't know how I got free in the end, but suddenly I was falling, and turned over several times in the air. Thank God! In my excitement I nearly operated the quick harness release instead of the cord, and at the last moment noticed that I was releasing the safety catch. Another shock! The parachute and I would have arrived separately, which would have done neither of us any good. A jerk, and like a pendulum I was suspended from the opened parachute. Slowly and softly I floated down to earth.

Below me a black column of smoke marked the spot where my machine had crashed. By rights I should have landed in the Forêt de Boulogne like a monkey on a tree, but the parachute only brushed a poplar and then folded up. Luckily, I landed in a soft, boggy meadow, and after the high tension of nerves and energy I had been under, collapsed immediately. I felt as wretched as a dog. Shot, and bleeding profusely from head and arm, with a painfully twisted ankle which at once started to swell, I could neither walk nor stand up. Suspicious and unfriendly French peasants came at last and carried me into a farmhouse. The first Germans I saw were men of the Todt Organisation from a nearby building site, who packed me into a car and took me back to my base at Audembert.

Everybody was already considerably worried about me, and my reception was correspondingly warm. After I had drunk an extra large cognac and smoked a cigar, essential after any kill, I felt much better. In the naval hospital at Hardinghem I was repaired by my good friend, Marine-Geschwaderarzt Dr Heim. I am especially grateful to him for allowing me to smoke on the operating table, and for not detaining me at the hospital, but letting me return to my base. I could continue to conduct operations from the ground, at least for the time being.

The news of the day's events–the Schlageter Group recorded a bag of 14–travelled fast, and congratulations poured in from all sides. My birthday and my seventieth kill were celebrated in a suitable manner. Osterkamp came over from Le Touquet, but what he had to tell me besides his congratulations struck me like a bolt from the blue–no one had expected anything like it, least of all myself. So far the Oak Leaves to the Knight's Cross had been the highest award for bravery, as far as we knew there was nothing higher to win in this war. Late the same night arrived the confirmation from the Führer's Headquarters: ' . . . I present you as the first officer of the German forces with the Oak Leaves with Swords to the Knight's Cross of the Iron Cross. Adolf Hitler!'

The Man in Action

Squadron Leader H. E. Bates is perhaps best remembered as Britain's finest modern short story writer. During the war, however, he distinguished himself as a pilot and also, under commission from the Government, in writing about life in the RAF. There are, in fact, few better novels of the war in the air than his *Fair Stood The Wind For France* (1944) and the short stories about the RAF he published under the pseudonym Flying Officer X. The following article was written for the American magazine, *Flying*, in September, 1942, and features another of the great Spitfire heroes, Squadron Leader A. C. Deere.

On a bright December afternoon a Stirling returning from a raid on the docks at Brest came into its aerodrome to land. Its pilot, an Australian, touched down with an exactitude that seemed to indicate that nothing extraordinary was wrong. He was within a day or two of his twenty-third birthday. His second pilot, contrary to the popular supposition that the pilots of bombers are for some reason middle-aged men, was a boy of 19. Among the crew was a young engineer, who was badly wounded. The floor of the plane was greasy with oil and blood and from the port outer engine a stream of petrol was pouring out like a bright fan in the wind. As the plane touched down it began to disintegrate. First the port outer propeller fell away; then the whole of the port inner engine. Then the complete port wing fell off and, falling, caught fire. The huge tyres of the Stirling were punctured and flat, and finally the whole aircraft tilted violently to port, flinging the starboard wing high into the air. The task of carrying a dying man from a plane which seemed at any moment about to blow up would, in civilian life, have been front page news; complete with pictures, personal interview and possibly framed certificates. Fortunately the plane did not blow up. Half an hour later its crew with the exception of the wounded engineer, now safely in hospital, were having tea, and of that extraordinary episode, and of the earlier episode in which the Stirling had beaten off the violent attacks of 10 Messerschmitts, there was nothing in the next morning's newspapers.

In this story and behind it, in ten thousand others of which the public will never see a record because there are so many of them, there is to be found a fraction of the picture that is being made, every day, every night, over sea and land and in all latitudes, of the men of the RAF in action. The title of these pictures is not heroism, since the RAF, with its vital genius for the rejection of normal speech and the coinage of new, does not know the word. Nor are they ever likely to occupy the place in popular literature and art long held by 'The Charge of the Light Brigade'. On the contrary they are, and will probably continue to be, taken very much for granted. For since the day when the British made the incredible and ghastly heroic blunder in the Crimea and somehow got it immortalized as a national epic, the standards of heroism, like the standards of speed and science and plain inhumanity, have undergone great changes. They have changed so far that they have, in some cases, ceased to mean anything. This has become very true of flying in general and, within the last three years, of the RAF in particular. One simple result of this is that the work of the RAF, which an earlier age would certainly have immortalised in verse, even if it was bad verse, is today recorded in language as plain, matter-of-fact and perishable as a cardboard box. The work of the RAF–words like deeds, exploits, feats of valour and so on have no place in its vocabulary–lies hidden too often behind colourless communiqués and factual broadcasts that we now take as much for granted as the kitchen stove.

For this flatness, the lack of the heroic touch in the history of its action achievement, the RAF is itself partly responsible. The men of the RAF are largely inarticulate; they would prefer anonymity; and perhaps the worst of all sins in the RAF is the process known as 'shooting a line'. The now immortal father of all line-shooters was a fighter pilot who was heard to declaim, with fine pomposity, in one of those unfortunate silences that sometimes fall on general conversation, 'There was I, flying upside down.' This remark has since become the standard by which any personal flying achievement in the RAF, whether heroic or not, has come to be judged. To shoot a line is now embarrassing, boring, comic, or in plain bad taste. In this way the RAF has elected to speak even of its most exceptional achievements in terms of understatement. To find the pilot who will tell you the story of a combat with simplicity, directness and lack of embarrassment is in consequence a rare thing.

To fly and to be inarticulate, even to pretend to be inarticulate, have become, with rare exceptions, inseparable qualities. To treat the daily association with danger as if it were nothing more than a game of cricket has become almost a rule. Laconic, nonchalant, dry, indifferent, the RAF passes a common verdict even on the most glorious of its moments of action with a couple of words. 'Good show,' it says. 'Good show.'

But what the RAF *does* and what the RAF *says* about what it does are necessarily different things. The fact that the achievements of the RAF have not so far been recorded with outstanding objectivity, force and imagination is due to very simple things. Pilots, for the most part, cannot write; writers, for the most part, cannot fly. The day on which we get a fusion of these qualities in one person we may be given, even though in a limited way, a real picture of the RAF in action. It will be limited not only because one pilot cannot speak for ten thousand, but because the fighter pilot differs from the bomber pilot and the bomber pilot in turn from the coastal pilot and all three in turn from the ferry pilot as much as the Spitfire from the Stirling, the Hampden from the Sunderland, the Liberator from the Kittyhawk. These types are not only temperamentally different from each other; their daily life is different; their actions and reactions are different; only their final aim, the destruction of an enemy, is the same. To understand them, to assess the differences in their lives and their performance in action, one must live with them for a long time.

Of all flying types the fighter pilot is, to the public, the most attractive. The reasons are again simple. His actions are seen as a triumph of individuality; he flies alone in a high-powered piece of mechanism which is capable, in his hands, of evolutions at great speed, of great beauty and spectacular effect. He is engaged in a dangerous, apparently wonderful and often fatal occupation. Like the bull-fighter, he works near to and often in line with death. To the public this near-fatal occupation, whether of bull-fighters, tight-rope walkers or fighter pilots, is fascinating to contemplate. For of all pilots the fighter pilot is most likely to be seen–and during the Battle of Britain was constantly seen–in action. The coastal pilot is invisible, far out at sea; the bomber pilot is invisible, far out in darkness. The Spitfire pilot flies in the sun, turning his plane like a silver fish many thousand feet up, and fascinates the world below.

This is one part of the picture; the finished, pleasant, spectacular part, seen by the public. There are two others. One is the daily and almost certainly boring routine of the aerodrome and the dispersal point, which the public never sees; the other is that of the action itself–which the public also rarely sees and which the combatant will rarely discuss, the action involving emotions, reactions and tension, for which the public has no remotely comparable experience of its own. The picture of life on the aerodrome is simple. On duty throughout all the daylight hours–as few as eight in winter, as many as 18 in summer– the fighter pilot's problem is often not how to kill Germans but how to kill time. His life, while waiting for action, may be intensely boring, dull, directionless. To counteract these things he reads, plays cards, revises navigation, talks shop. His action, even when it comes, is packed into a hundred minutes, of which perhaps 10 or 15 form the vortex in which he destroys or is destroyed.

From the thousands of stories by the fighters in action it is not possible to select one which will typify the fighter pilot. It is simpler to select a man who has crowded into one life the experience of 20 pilots and to record of him simply–'This is not typical. It belongs to the highest and rarest achievement. But it happened.'

Of all fighter pilots Squadron Leader A. C. Deere, DFC and bar, is probably least typical. He was born in New Zealand; joined the RAF in 1937; won service boxing championships; played football. In four months of the summer of 1940, from May to August, he destroyed 17 enemy planes. He was shot down seven times; baled out three times. He collided head-on with an enemy machine; a pupil pilot cut his Spitfire in two. One plane of his was once blown 150 yards along the ground by a bomb; another blew up three seconds after he left it.

His action began in May, 1940. He had volunteered, with another pilot, to escort a small training-type aircraft to Marck, the aerodrome at Calais. He was to land there and pick up a squadron leader who had force-landed. The Battle of France was in progress; Calais was surrounded by the enemy; the aerodrome was a kind of 'No-man's land'. When the trainer landed, the passenger was nowhere to be seen. After waiting a few moments the trainer took off again and was just airborne when a dozen Me 109s attacked the escort planes. The trainer, forced back to land, hit a hedge. Then followed what Deere himself has described as 'a grand shooting match with the Me's'–the words are typical–leaving Deere and his fellow pilot still flying and the wrecks of Messerschmitts lying all about the beach, the aerodrome and the town. The action seems to have been a fine example of the gay ferocity for which fighter pilots have become famous: Deere claimed two certainly destroyed and one probable, his companion one certainty and two probables. The pilot of the trainer got away.

From that moment Deere seems to have had no rest. His patrols over the coast of France began at 3.45 a.m.; often he made two before breakfast. In a few days his squadron lost six pilots; and soon Deere, although only a pilot officer, had become its leader. His adventures began to be fantastic. When he pursued a Dornier from Dunkirk to Ostend and both the Dornier and his own machine crash-landed, Deere was knocked out and his machine began to burn. As he scrambled clear, half conscious, his machine exploded. Two days later he collided with an Me 109 in mid-air. Each pilot seems to have thought that the other would give way. They passed each other once, turned and came together again. Deere lost a little height in the second turn and the belly of the Me tore along the fuselage of his plane, running the hood down on his head. The propeller was snapped off by this impact and the engine partially torn out. Deere, blinded by smoke and flames, could see nothing and could only hold the plane in a 100 mph glide which took him gradually over the English coast. There his craft hit a concrete anti-invasion post, ripped off a wing, skidded through two cornfields and finally burnt up.

A week or two later he chased a Heinkel over the

Channel towards Calais. Shooting down the Heinkel, he was immediately 'jumped on by a swarm of other fighters'. A bullet ripped the watch from his wrist; another scorched an eyebrow. His aircraft was full of holes, and over Ashford, 20 miles inland and at 800 feet, it began to fall to pieces. Those were the days when shoppers in that market town in the heart of the Kentish sheep and hop and orchard country would look up 20 times a day–I myself among them–and watch the battles in the blue summer air. They must have watched with horror that day as Deere baled out of his disintegrating plane, his parachute not opening until he was perilously close to the earth. Yet Deere was flying again next day.

Two days later he had his oil tank shot away and had to force-land without his air speed indicator; soon afterwards his rudder was shot away and his engine set on fire. He baled out again and landed in a plum tree. Next morning his aerodrome was dive-bombed. A bomb fell immediately in front of him as he sat in his plane, blew the engine of the Spitfire out and sent the plane itself hurtling upside down with Deere in it, for 150 yards. He was helped out by a fellow pilot and ran for shelter. Afterwards he was put to bed and was still in bed, next day, when another raid began. He got up from his bed immediately, went up in his Spitfire and shot down a Dornier.

Shortly afterwards he was teaching tactics to a pupil. Something went wrong; the pupil collided with the teacher, cutting the Spitfire in half. Deere was caught in the wreckage of his plane and could not jump. The plane fell for several thousand feet before he could get clear. Half of his parachute harness had been torn off; the rip cord dangled out of his reach. Deere closed his eyes and waited, knowing there was nothing he could do. Suddenly his shoulders were violently jerked by the parachute opening of its own accord. That day Deere was in hospital for the third time.

A large part of these adventures cannot be called heroic; they are examples of fantastic misfortunes which may and do happen to any pilot, any day, anywhere. Deere's career is remarkable because he brings to such a succession of events, any one of which might have been his death, an indomitable stoicism; the spirit of apparently careless fatalism which is an important part of the fighter pilot's make-up. Above all he brings to them, as almost every pilot does, a passion for flying.

The Battle of Dieppe

Flying Officer H. H. Strickland was one of the group of Americans who came to Britain before their own country entered the war and flew with the famous Eagle Squadron of Spitfires. Here he gives a vivid account of how the Allied Forces began the strike back into Europe which was to lead to the eventual downfall of Germany.

Because of the right combination of weather, wind and the moon we knew that conditions were right, and we knew that a large combined operation had been planned for some time; but it was not until the afternoon of August 18, 1942, that we knew exactly where and when the battle would occur.

On the afternoon of the 18th we saw Group Captain John Peel arrive at the forward station to which we had been sent; he was carrying an armful of maps and a long list of orders. We pilots were taken into the intelligence room, and the group captain addressed us there.

'This is IT!' whispered O'Regan soon after the group captain began to speak.

The Commanding Officer explained the general plan of attack. On a large map he pointed to the coastal area– Berneval, Dieppe, St. Marguerite. He showed us the emplacements on the flanks that the Commandos would attack, and he showed where the South Saskatchewan

Regiment and the Cameroons would make the frontal assault. After the group captain had finished Wing Commander Duke-Woolley then described the specific tasks for the wing as a whole and for each squadron. 71 Squadron's part was easy to understand: we were to maintain air protection near the shoreline and prevent air attacks on our frontal assault forces.

That meant we would be in the thick of it. And that suited us.

After our commanders had finished, everyone was ordered to remain on the post. Telephonic communications were discontinued.

Some very heavy dates at 'The Swan', 'The Ship' and other spots cracked up pretty badly that Tuesday night.

We rose early next morning and hurried to breakfast. We knew that during the day the Luftwaffe would meet us with strong fighter strength. We knew that the staffels, the German fighter squadrons, at Abbeville, Amiens, St. Omer, Le Havre and Antwerp would join battle. We knew, too, that these fighters were some of the Hun's absolute best; he had kept his aces on the Western front to meet the sweeps that the RAF and the American Air Force were continually sending over. We were certain that during the day we would meet the Luftwaffe, and that suited us plenty. We had been trying for a long time to make Jerry come up and fight. With a show like this big raid striking at him, he would simply have to get off the ground.

When we started the Merlin engines of our Spitfires, some cloud patches had piled up in the east, making it very dark. We pointed our Spits into the breeze in tight formation of fours, and took off into the night, then we quickly shifted to line astern. We flew low over Kent on our way out, and, still flying almost on the deck, we arrived at our departure point on the English coast. Then we set our course for Dieppe, flying very low and close to the sea. Each of us watched his instruments carefully, for in the dark there was no horizon and the sea was flat.

It was still dark when we arrived to cover the dawn landing. Our troops were already ashore and were fighting hard. And the heavy guns of both forces were firing steadily; they were feeling for their targets. Whenever one of the big guns on shore hit one of our boats, we could see the flames leap up and sometimes there would be an explosion. From where we were up above, we could spot the shrapnel bursts and the almost continuous streaks of red Bofors projectiles, rising and converging toward our Hurricane bombers that were ahead of us and flying low, making absolutely point-blank attacks against the German gun posts, trying to knock them out so they could not operate against our troops that had already landed and those that were coming in to land.

Just as the first light of day was breaking, and the protective cover of darkness was disappearing, a bomber from our side skimmed in with his belly almost touching the water, and laid a smoke screen across the harbour. A very light wind drifted it towards the cliffs and into the eyes of the German gunners who were firing from there.

From the sea hundreds of our corvettes, transports, destroyers, troop and tank transports, minesweepers, trawlers and rescue boats were deployed. Those nearest shore were advancing doggedly through the Hun mine-fields and a strong artillery barrage. From time to time one of them was hit and exploded. Whenever there was an explosion, the boat disappeared below the water under a cloud of spray and foam, leaving an oil slick. Over the whole of the battle area there hung a thickening pall of smoke from the cordite, the smoke screens, distress flares, and exploding shells.

Our naval artillery action was having a particularly good effect. This barrage was gradually silencing enemy positions. High up above we could sit in the cockpits of our Spitfires and look down, and we noticed a slackening in the numbers of huge geysers that had been rising

105

among our numerous sea craft. The enemy's primary resistance was slowly being overcome by our naval guns and by the attack of the Commandos themselves, who were capturing a number of positions in hand-to-hand fighting. As darkness changed into daylight, we could see that our fellows were advancing against the harbour's fortifications. We could also see that our troops were filtering throughout the town by means of hard street fighting. I can tell you it made us feel mighty good as we stooged around upstairs looking down and watching those troops advance into the teeth of all the Germans could throw at them. It was pretty darn exciting, and I reckon I was seeing one of the best shows any man has ever seen; it was mighty spectacular.

Curiously, our squadron did not encounter strong fighter opposition on that first sortie, and this lack of fighter resistance over the principal landing area surprised us a lot; we had expected the Germans to come up immediately and give strong opposition as soon as they realized the size of the combined attack we were launching. But in this initial stage of the battle, the enemy fighters which did rise were few in number, and they attacked in a very half-hearted manner. Only one of our chaps–it was Strickland–got a shot at a Focke-Wulf 190. He damaged it, and the other Huns near by were so jittery they promptly whipped about and fled.

It was well after sunrise when this first sortie drew to its close, and we turned toward the sea, headed for home. We made our landfall, then steered for base, flying low over the beautiful hills and fields of Kent. The country lanes around Canterbury and Tunbridge Wells, winding among valleys, were filling with ground fog. We were glad that our drome was on a hilltop.

Before our propellers stopped turning, our splendid ground crew went into action, quickly refuelling, re-arming and inspecting our craft. We learnt that Morgan had crash-landed with a glycol leak near Beachy Head, coming down alongside a burning Blenheim.

We pilots agreed that while enemy coastal resistance at Dieppe might be lessened when next we went over, we knew that air resistance would be increased. We knew that Jerry would simply have to come and give us fight. He could not sit at home on his duff while a show like this was going on. Hence we gulped our coffee and prepared for the second sortie.

As we were going out the second time, when we were about 20 miles off shore, we passed some of our sea craft returning with the first batch of the wounded.

When we approached Dieppe this time, we saw great fires and high columns of smoke rising: the harbour, the Casino and some of the hotels that once were so famous at this resort were now blazing, while ammunition dumps were blowing up here and there. It was quickly apparent that our main forces had landed effectively, and had spread far afield. The work of the demolition squads was particularly apparent: they had blasted a number of buildings, and from time to time another would rise up into the air, shudder for an instant, then splatter. It was great fun to watch the demolition boys do their work.

As we were flying over Dieppe we were informed in the air that the Canadians had captured the racetrack, and that it was available as an emergency field if any of us had to crash-land.

This time when we arrived there were plenty of enemy aircraft in the air. As we approached the battle area we could see an absolute swirl of twisting aeroplanes. One hell of a big battle was going on in the air as well as on the ground.

Even before we got within range of the fighting, we heard the calm voice of the Controller-on-the-spot, the Commander who was directing the fighting from the air, say, 'Get that Dornier! Get him before he attacks that ship.' Then we saw the Spitfires dive for him, and they literally blew him out of the sky, exploding him with cannon shell and sending him down in pieces.

Then Duke-Woolley, our wingco, came in: 'Warming up, chaps!' which meant we were to pour on the coal, to speed up and make ready for the attack. We split into three columns of fours. Blue Section, in which I was fighting, was ordered to climb toward a formation of Focke-Wulf 190s. We went for them, twisting and turning like an angry snake, manœuvring and counter-manœuvring with the 190s. But we soon saw they didn't actually want to fight; they just wanted to draw us away from the west flank of our convoy, thus exposing our ships to the bombers who were hovering around, waiting for a chance to get over the convoy and drop their bombs.

A Ju 88 did manage to get through our high cover and come in. Pete, our CO who was leading White Section, immediately spoke over the R/T: 'Hurry up! Get that 88.'

Right away we saw Red Section begin firing at the bomber. And we saw White Section, with Pete in front, almost standing their Spitfires on their tails as they came in terrifically fast from below. We in Blue Section had given up playing tag with the Focke-Wulf 190s and we, too, were trying to get within range, but finally we reluctantly gave up the chase with the Hun bomber hell-bent for Berlin, black smoke streaming from its engines and some 15 Spitfires on its tail, each of them trying to get into position to make the kill.

During this period of high-speed manœuvring, we had to ignore the anti-aircraft guns, and we actually flew through our own barrage twice. Flak from our own surface ships burst very close but fortunately none of us was hit.

We were all twisting and weaving like mad because the Germans were attacking from above, coming in as fast as a bomb, simply whizzing past us, firing as they went. Sometimes they were in range and gone before we even saw them. But sometimes we saw them coming and managed to fire a burst as they went past. In all this fighting many planes were shot down. And we of the Eagle Squadron, all of us Americans, were particularly cheered by the news that American Flying Fortresses with all-American crews had gone over that morning and knocked out the Abbeville drome, rendering it useless to the enemy during the day, forcing him to base his fighters at some more distant field. One of the boys who had flown over the Abbeville drome said it wasn't anything but a bloody great hole; he said the Fortresses had simply wrecked it. We Americans were almighty proud of that.

By this time the air battle was nearing its maximum intensity.

It reached that maximum as our third sortie arrived off Dieppe. We got there just in time for the fiercest combat of the day, just as our forces were beginning to withdraw.

This was the time, of course, for which the Luftwaffe had been waiting because the concentration of troops at the time of withdrawal would present the Hun his best target of the day. After having spent more than nine hours ashore our Commandos and shock troops were coming out, and the Germans were flying everything they had to make the attack. Ju 88s and additional Dorniers were brought up. Squadrons of German fighters had been brought from far distances. The air was simply filled with planes marked with the Maltese cross and the swastika.

The Red, White and Blue sections of Eagle Squadron were terribly busy. We attacked again and again, attacking the German fighters and shooting our way through to get at the bombers that were being escorted out to bomb our ships. The Eagles that day shot down two bombers and damaged a number of others. Gus Daymond's Red Section of four Spitfires attacked a formation of 15 190s and simply chased them out of the sky, Gus calling to them over the R/T and telling them they were yellow sons-of-a-bitch not to stay and fight.

Our successes were sadly overbalanced when we heard that Squadron Leader Peterson had been shot down. Pete had last been seen closing in on a Ju 88 until he was at point-blank range and then letting the bomber have it. But in the fight the German tail gunner managed to get in a burst that blasted Pete's machine and he called out over the R/T that he was baling out. I felt my guts sort of tighten in me when I heard old Pete saying he had been hit and was hopping out into the drink.

It seemed we were getting our bad luck all at once because it wasn't long before I heard Mike McPharlin crying out for a homing, for directions as to how to get back to England. Then pretty soon he said there wasn't any bloody good in giving him any directions, that he was out of petrol and he was stepping overboard.

I felt mighty unhappy as I turned back home after this sortie and headed for England, knowing that two of my best pals were struggling down there in the Channel somewhere below me. I looked down at the sea and everything I saw on the water I imagined was Pete or Mike. Anyhow I sincerely hoped it was and that they hadn't had any bad luck, got tangled in their chute harness, or their dinghy had been punctured, or any bad luck like that.

We were refuelling and re-arming for the fourth sortie when the Air Officer Commanding sent the signal, 'Though I know you are tired from a long day of fighting, I request that maximum effort be exerted for a few more hours. A great Air Victory is in sight!'

We gulped some more tea, and swallowed some more sandwiches, which the Waafs kept prepared throughout the long day. We took off quickly, and the wing, Duke-Woolley still leading, steered again for Dieppe.

About mid-Channel we met our forces, homeward bound now with the wounded ahead, the damaged craft immediately behind, and the navy deployed far behind, patrolling and guarding the rear.

The Wing Commander held us in a fairly tight wing formation. Enemy fighters were about. A squadron of them appeared. Gus Daymond, now that Pete had been shot down, was leading 71. Always looking for a fight, Gus manœuvred us for the attack, but the 190s would not accept the challenge. They made only a feeble attempt to harass us, and once more Gussie screamed his contempt of yellow bastards who flew around the sky just to look pretty and wouldn't fight.

We did not know at this time that some two hundred and fifty of the German fighters and bombers had been destroyed, probably destroyed, or damaged. We did not know that the vaunted Luftwaffe had suffered a telling and most humiliating defeat.

From up above we looked down and watched our convoy pushing its way homeward. Minesweepers were far out in front. Corvettes were twisting around, leaving queer patterns in their wake. Rescue launches were speeding about in search of pilots in the drink. I was thankful that the sea was calm and as I flew in formation, weaving and twisting and watching for enemy fighters, I still had time to wonder about Pete and Mike.

Low clouds and rain squalls were approaching from the direction of the Isle of Wight. The sun was sinking fast, and we knew that soon the ships below would be alongside the cliffs of England and under full protection of darkness.

Remnants of Luftwaffe fighter staffels still circled very high above us, but none of them would come down and fight. They stayed far out of range, just perched in the sky, slowly circling like birds with outstretched wings riding the high currents.

It was dusk when we finally glided into our small drome near the Thames after our last patrol. Not knowing we weren't going out again, the mechanics quickly re-armed and refuelled while we stood by in readiness, waiting to be ordered out once more. But even before darkness had completely enveloped the Estuary and the coast of Kent, it was apparent that for the remainder of the nineteenth

111

day of August the crack staffels were incapable of further effort. Any further bombing attacks by them could be handled by the RAF's normal complement of night fighters.

We were finally released off the station with a signal of congratulations from the Air Marshall.

Eagle pilots move fast when released by operations. To us 'release' means 'vamoose'. Thus, it was not very long until, by devious routes through the blackout, we all arrived, a tired bunch, at 'The Black Swan'.

Most of us were there having some pretty long drinks when the message came through: 'Squadron Leader Peterson and Flying Officer McPharlin saved from the Channel and well!'

I can tell you that our cheers fairly lifted the roof–almost as high as our big naval guns had lifted those German buildings that day back in Dieppe. We were mighty glad to know that good old Pete and Mike were out of the drink and safe.

Death of An Ace

Pilot Officer F. A. Aikman, a young Canadian airman who flew as 'No. 2' to the legendary Irish fighter pilot, Wing Commander Brendan E. Finucane (32 'kills'), describes the tragic end to his skipper's brilliant career in the summer of 1942 . . .

'This is it, chaps!' These were the last words, spoken in a quiet, self-possessed voice by Wing Commander Brendan 'Paddy' Finucane, Fighter Command's 21 year-old ace pilot and my 'No. 1', just before he crashed into the sea off the coast of France on July 15, 1942.

It was not the Luftwaffe who ended the career of this splendid young Irishman who, in two years' fighting, had shot down at least 32 enemy planes. To the end he was unbeaten in aerial combat.

It was a 'million-to-one chance' shot from a German machine-gun on the beach near Pointe du Touquet that finished him. At the time he was leading our Spitfire wing during the largest mass attack yet carried out by fighter pilots on targets in France. It was also the cruellest of blows, because 'Paddy' had only just been promoted to Wing Commander the previous month.

I was 'No. 2' on that ill-fated mission. And by a curious twist of fate 'Paddy' had only been talking to me about his feelings as a fighter pilot before we took off. I can

113

recall his words as clearly as when he spoke them.

'Before going on a trip I usually have a funny feeling in my tummy,' he admitted, 'but once I'm in my aircraft everything is fine. The brain is working fast, and if the enemy is met it seems to work like a clockwork motor. Accepting, rejecting, sizing up, and remembering.

'You don't have time to feel anything. But your nerves may be on edge–not from fear, but from excitement and the intensity of the mental effort. I have come back from a sweep to find my tunic wet through with perspiration.'

He also talked about how he felt after a battle. 'Chaps sometimes find that they can't sleep,' he said. 'What happens is this. You come back from a show and find it very hard to remember what happened. Maybe you have a clear impression of three or four incidents, which stand out like illuminated lantern slides in the mind's eye. Perhaps a picture of two Me 109s belting down on your tail from out of the sun and already within firing range.

'Perhaps another picture of your cannon shells striking the belly of an Me and the aircraft spraying debris around. But for the life of you, you can't remember what you did.

'Later, when you have turned in and sleep is stealing over you, some tiny link in the chain of events comes back. Instantly you are fully awake, and then the whole story of the operation pieces itself together and you lie there, sleep driven away, re-living the combat, congratulating yourself for this thing, blaming yourself for that.

'The reason for this is simply that everything happens so quickly in the air that you crowd a tremendous amount of thinking, action and emotion into a very short space of time, and you suffer afterwards from mental indigestion!'

Perhaps strangest of all, 'Paddy' also spoke at that time about the possibility of death. 'The tactical side of the game is quite fascinating,' he smiled ruefully. 'You get to learn, for instance, how to fly so that all the time you have a view behind you as well as in front. The first necessity in combat is to see the other chap before he sees you, or at least before he gets the tactical advantage of you. The second is to hit him when you fire. You mightn't have a second chance.'

But there was certainly no thought in my mind that my Commander might not return from the mission when we set off for France that July day.

I remember that we were flying at zero feet right down on the deck. And as we flew over the beach, I saw a small machine-gun post perched about 20 feet above the beach on a ridge of sand.

We were almost on the post before 'Paddy' realised it was there, and the soldiers opened up at point-blank range. The first burst went through 'Paddy's' starboard wing and radiator.

I was flying behind him and to the right, and as I went in I took a crack at the gun-post. When the dust had settled down a little there was nothing to be seen on the sand, and I guessed my fire blew that post to blazes.

But 'Paddy' did not know he had been hit, for he pulled up a little to fly over the post. I called him up on the rado: 'You have had it, sir, in your radiator.'

He then called out, 'I shall have to get out of this. Hello. Wing Commander calling. I have had it. Am turning out.'

He went into a turn, and then flew out on a reciprocal course. I was flying close to him, and I could see him clearly in the cockpit. He opened his sliding hood, and just before he crashed, I saw him take off his helmet. He was doing something else in the cockpit. Releasing his parachute harness, I should say.

When the Spitfire hit the deck, I thought it might stay afloat for a few seconds. Long enough for him to get out. But it sank like a stone, carrying 'Paddy' with it. The impact must have knocked him unconscious.

We circled the sea for a long time after that. But all we saw was a slowly-widening streak of oil which floated on the dark waters of the Channel . . .

Dogfight!

Flight Lieutenant Richard Hillary was another of the legendary young Spitfire aces, and his book, *The Last Enemy* (1942), remains to this day one of the most famous works about the Second World War. In it he vividly recorded his meteorlike life and the terrible crash in the English Channel when he was 21 which left him terribly burned. Hillary also gave a series of four radio talks about the airman's war in August, 1941, though, curiously, he remained anonymous. Explaining the reason for this, his friend, the author Eric Linklater, wrote, 'A nameless young man, invisible in the studio, could describe his battles over the Channel in a quiet, impersonal way–but the stories must not be attached to a Flying Officer whose face and hands bore the horrid scars of reality. That would be propaganda . . .' I have managed to locate one of these evocative talks and here it is.

In this war, by far the most vivid memories are not those of fierce fighting, or firing guns or flying aeroplanes–they are of quiet moments at the beginning and end of each day when dawn is breaking or night falls. Some of the sunrises that I have seen have been among the most beautiful moments that I can remember.

It was just growing light. Our Spitfires were standing looking slim and eager to get into the air. There was no wind; a white mist was drifting over the Thames Estuary and it was rather chilly and damp.

But then in no time we were airborne, packed in tight formation. Already in the east the sun was rising over the North Sea. It was all so strangely beautiful, and yet, ever present, was the thought of the grim and dangerous work soon to be done.

Our job was to patrol at 20,000 feet to stop the German Messerschmitt fighters from protecting the bombers below. Underneath us, three squadrons were to deal with the bombers. Above us, another squadron of Spitfires patrolled.

We flew straight into the sun on the way over, and I could see very little as my eyes watered with the strain of looking for the enemy.

For 35 minutes we flew around the coast of France, when suddenly we saw black dots a little to the north-east of us. We rushed towards them, and in a moment the sky was full of whirling aircraft, diving, twisting and turning. Too late, both squadrons realised that we were friends, and although we had not opened fire at one another, it was going to be impossible to form up again in our own squadrons.

Round and round we went looking for our sections. I noticed queer little straight lines of smoke very close together as I flew past them. Suddenly I woke up.

'Someone is shooting; it's smoke from incendiary bullets!' I told myself. I gave up all thought of trying to find the rest of the squadron and started searching all round.

Then there they were flying across my front–two Me 109s! They turned towards me, and went into a steep climbing turn. Up the two of them went. How they could climb! They were level with me about 400 yards away; another one joined them. I could see no other aeroplanes by now–just the three 109s.

It was a question of who could get the most height first. I opened the throttle as far as it would go. I was gaining a little now, and with my more manoeuvrable Spitfire I could turn inside the 109s. Slowly, in giant spirals, we gained height, and suddenly I found myself up-sun of all three of them. I quickly turned the other way, and they lost me.

Round I came at 26,000 feet, and I was right behind the last 109–but too far away to shoot yet. I gained–oh, so slowly!–but sure enough, I was gaining. How long could I wait before firing or before the leader saw me? He was weaving about pretty violently now, looking for me.

At last, I was in range of the 109. I pressed the button, and my whole aeroplane shuddered as the eight guns fired. Nothing happened. The German flew on.

Then suddenly there was a flash, and the enemy aircraft flicked over: his port aileron had been hit and had come off. He jettisoned his hood to jump out and I turned quickly when showers of tracer bullets flew past me. I had forgotten the other two Me 109s!

Instantly I flicked over into a turn, dived for the cloud cover, and thankfully lost them. It had been close! Now time was getting on and I knew I had not much petrol left. It was time to go home.

At last my aerodrome came in sight. I landed just as another plane was taxiing-in. By ten o'clock three more pilots had returned, making five in all, and we sat down to a terrific breakfast of bacon and eggs and champagne (the chef had produced the champagne!).

One by one the squadron came back. Practically everyone had shot something down, and many had been damaged slightly. There were only two pilots missing, and our squadron score was 10 destroyed, three probables, and three damaged.

Sadly, we never heard of those missing men again.

The Fighter Pilot's Paradise

After the Spitfire's crucial role in the Battle of Britain–and then its invaluable help in the Allies' march back into Europe–the plane was next put into operation in several of the other theatres of war. In the years which followed it again distinguished itself in such farflung places as Malta, North Africa, Sicily, Singapore, Burma and even in Australian skies, where it was a keen foe for the Japanese Zeros. From the numerous reports covering these areas, I have selected two typical items by famous writers which particularly stress the dedication and good humour of Spitfire pilots.

The story of Malta's indomitable resistance to the Germans is well known, and a crucial factor in this battle against almost impossible odds was the arrival in the summer of 1942 of a squadron of Spitfires. Among the pilots was Squadron Leader George 'Screwball' Beurling, an extraordinary Canadian whose highly individual skills were to earn him a record 31 enemy 'kills' during the war. A great admirer of Beurling was Wing Commander Pierre Clostermann, himself an air ace and also author of the classic book, *The Big Show*. Here Wing Commander Clostermann gives us a delightful account of 'Screwball's' eventful arrival in 'The Fighter Pilot's Paradise' on June 9, 1942 . . .

HMS *Eagle*, escorted by two destroyers, pressed ahead and left behind the British convoy bound for Malta. It was 5 a.m., just before sunrise. The carrier's deck was covered with Spitfire Vs equipped with auxiliary tanks.

The pilots gave their planes a final check over. They

119

were Spit V-Cs ('tropical') armed with four 20 mm cannon. They were at least brand-new planes, and at a time when everyone, from Moscow to London, from Australia to Alaska, from Libya to the Caribbean, was screaming for fighters the pilots felt they had not done too badly to get them.

All the same, they were slightly nervous–not one of them had ever taken off from a carrier. While they strapped themselves in, the fitters finished stowing their meagre possessions in the magazines of the machine-guns and of two of the cannon–the other two cannon were loaded. Over the Tannoy came the naval flight-officer's final instructions: navigation gen, courses, ETAs, frequencies, etc.

At 6.05 a.m. the first Spitfire took off. Pointing his yellow flag, the deck officer signalled Beurling to get under way. This was it. Rather tensed, he slowly opened the throttle while keeping the brakes hard on. As soon as the tail lifted and the Spit began to champ at the bit, he let her go. Drawn by its 1500 hp engine, and with a 30 mph headwind and the ship's own 20 knots helping, the plane was airborne almost immediately.

By 6.30 the last Spit had taken off and the *Eagle* immediately turned about. The Algerian coast was only thirty miles away, and there might be enemy submarines lurking around. Already in formation, the 32 planes receded in the distance, heading east on their flight to Malta.

The sea was blue, without a wrinkle. To the right was the violet line of the Tunisian coast, down below the white patch formed by the island of Lampedusa, over there to the left at the foot of that thundercloud forming was Sicily, with its 14 airfields crammed with Messerschmitts.

More and more frequently, as Malta drew nearer, snatches of conversation came over the R/T. Interference from German radio-location also began to jingle in the pilots' ears like an antique telephone bell.

The formation was flying at 24,000 feet and the cold was intense in spite of the sun. Fifteen minutes to go. Malta called:

'Hullo, Condor leader, this is Timber calling. Steer 081 and get a move on. Do not answer. Repeat, do not answer. Out.'

Things must be hotting up, and Woodhall, the controller, getting anxious. He had no doubt seen on his radar screen an enemy raid forming over Sicily. It was probably going to develop into a race, if the Luftwaffe were not to catch them with their pants down as they landed, for the Germans had cathode-ray tubes too.

Malta ahead! A big grey and green oval, perched on white cliffs resting on the sea, and flanked to the north-west by the two small islands of Comino and Gozo.

The formation split up into sections of four, diving separately. Details became discernible—the seething bay of Marsa Xlokh, the deep gash of Valetta harbour, ringed by tiers of flat-roofed houses, the web of hedges and stone walls cutting up the arid fields. Further on, the leprous sore of the main airfield, riddled with bomb craters.

Beurling had pushed back his hood and, while the first sections, with their flaps and undercarts down, were joining the circuit, he had a good look round.

Accustomed to the orderly arrangement of English airfields, he was taken aback at the sight of this stretch of ground, five miles long, with bits of runway everywhere and sinuous tracks disappearing into underground shelters. This extraordinary airfield was really three—Luqa, Safi and Hal Far—connected by two gravel strips, so that in effect a plane could take off or land anywhere, i.e. on whichever the last enemy raid had left intact.

However serious the damage, there was always some serviceable corner left. Enormous heaps of stones were dotted here and there, for filling in the new craters as soon as the raid was over. All round the perimeter, except where it ran along the cliff, there was a series of bays with thick walls, to protect parked planes from splinters. Remains of burnt-out wings and fuselages were scattered about everywhere.

Six Spitfires took off to cover the newcomers' landing. The field was swarming with men. Beurling did not quite know where to land. In the end he just followed the others down and found himself on a bumpy track at the end of which stood a group of soldiers waving him on. As he came past, two of them grabbed hold of his wing-tips while a third jumped on the wing and caught hold of his shoulder. Through the wind from the propeller this one yelled into his ear that he had better hurry up, Jerry was on the way.

In the end he found himself in a kind of rabbit burrow formed by heaps of petrol cans filled with sand. Before he had time to draw breath he was surrounded by a gesticulating crowd of extraordinary-looking individuals, unshaven and dressed in relics of the uniforms of all three Services. The fitter who had guided him in switched his engine off. Three muscular types grabbed the tail and swung the plane round so that it faced the airfield again. More men came staggering up with cans of petrol.

Beurling, flabbergasted, was ejected from his seat by a pilot who promptly took his place. Trying to keep out of the way of all these madmen he found himself in a slit trench at the back of the burrow. All his goods and chattels, lovingly stowed away in the wings, were sent flying in every direction.

'Get a move on, get a move on!' Everybody seemed to be shouting the same thing. The armourers came up at the double, screwdrivers between their teeth and festooned with belts of shells and cartridges. The radio-fitter had already clapped on his earphones, opened the fuselage panels, changed the crystals in the set and checked the battery terminals. The empty oxygen-bottle was changed for a full one, all ready waiting in the corner.

The pilot was getting impatient and drumming on the

fuselage. Beurling, not quite knowing what to do, mechanically lit a cigarette. It was immediately snatched out of his mouth by a type who, before he had time to protest, bawled something at him and rushed back to his job. He might have known better; petrol was being brought up by a chain of soldiers and poured in the open through a large lined funnel.

The auxiliary tank was whisked off the plane.

'Hurry up, for Christ's sake!'

Already in the distance they could hear the Bofors batteries opening up. Bang, bang, bang, bang, bang–the five barks from one charger–bang! bang! bang! bang! bang! The Jerries must have arrived.

The ground-crew worked on frantically. From all over the field came the roar of Merlin engines starting up.

'OK? Contact!'

The men sprang off the Spitfire as it too started up, raising a furious wind which picked up Beurling's trampled shirts and underclothes and flung them into the air.

The pilot took the aircraft out of the bay with savage bursts of throttle which made the rudder vibrate. Still flat on one wing was an armourer, hanging on to the leading edge with one hand while he screwed down the last machine-gun panel with the other. Just as the Spit opened up, he let go everything and rolled on to the ground, only just escaping being bashed in by the tail-plane.

Beurling was now alone. The crowd of madmen had vanished into thin air. He emerged from his hole and made for the open. He ran into three other pilots from the *Eagle*, just as dazed as himself, who dragged him along in a frantic rush for a shelter. It was high time. The air vibrated with the powerful rumbling roar of a big formation very high up, and the shriller sound of Spitfires attacking. The staccato crackle of the machine-guns stood out above the muffled boom-boom-boom of the 20 mm Hispano cannon.

Look out! He just had time to turn round and see six

Messerschmitt 109s, which had sneaked in low over the water, jump Hal Far cliff and streak across the field at 400 mph with all guns blazing.

It was Beurling's first glimpse of a 109. In France, when he was on 222 Squadron, he had met only Focke-Wulf 190s.

One of the 109s passed within ten yards of him, and the deafening roar of his engine mingled with the whine of the 40 mm shells from the AA, firing horizontally and spraying the ground with splinters.

Just at that moment Beurling was sent flying head first into a trench by a push from one of his mates. He raised his head. The Junkers 88s–about 50 of them, escorted by 60 Messerschmitt 109s–were starting their dive. They were peeling off one by one and coming down in a 65-degree dive on the airfield in one unbroken line. The deep tone of the engines had changed to a screaming crescendo. The earth quivered, and sand trickled into the trenches. Bombs ripped down with a noise like an express train. The 88s flattened out at 1500 feet, their glass-house noses and their elongated nacelles clearly visible.

The bombs exploded with a terrifying crump, great clods of earth flew up, splinters whizzed murderously, mowing down everything in their path. Each explosion sent a shock wave through the earth and each time Beurling felt a thump like a kick in the stomach.

The empty cases of the 20 mm fell like hail, clanging against the empty cans. A Junkers 88, hit, continued its dive and crashed with a tremendous roar between two parked Wellingtons, which immediately burst into flame. Clouds of dust rose, mixed with smoke. The air stank of hot metal, sulphur and cordite. Shell splinters rained down.

A muffled explosion, followed by two others–another Junkers 88 had crashed, the wreck bouncing along in a sheet of flame.

Four parachutes hung above, stupidly silent amidst the

infernal din.

A minute's relative calm on the ground while the battle raged 10,000 feet up. Planes circled in pairs, pursuer and pursued; wings glinted in the sun, and all the time the rattle of machine-guns went on. Now and then a plane broke away from the mêlée, trailing white smoke–over there, a Spitfire, and that ball of fire plummeting into the sea was a Messerschmitt 109.

The sky was thick with black clusters of AA bursts–like lumps of coal thrown up by the Bofors batteries.

A new wave of bombers came cascading down. Two Junkers 88s, harried by Spitfires and both with engines on fire, broke from the line and dived towards the sea.

Very high in the sky, well above all the turmoil, five little bright dots could be seen in impeccable formation. They were five Italian Cants. Nobody took any notice of them, but their perfectly grouped stick of bombs fell plumb on the intersection of the two runways on Safi airfield. How those bombs managed to fall through all those whirling planes without smashing a single one was a miracle.

The newly arrived pilots, covered with dust and rubble, shaken by the exploding bombs, huddling down to avoid the hail of stones and splinters, were rocked to their foundations. This really was war! Ten minutes later it was all over. The Spitfires, fuel running low and ammunition spent, came into the circuit to land. Five Hurricanes from Takali airfield at the other end of the island flew above Luqa to protect the landing and the hurried dispersal of the planes. Beurling went back to his rabbit burrow to look for his belongings and wait for his plane to come back. He failed to find his razor or his toothbrush, which must have been left behind somewhere in the wings.

The planes were now coming in. Two with damaged undercarts had to belly-land, while a third with a good square yard of wing missing did a ground loop and turned a. over t. Just about one plane in three was obviously damaged in one way or another. A promising look-out!

A pilot who came past, exhausted and eyes bloodshot, and humping his parachute, called across,

'No point waiting for your Spit. Norman Lee was flying it and he got the chop. Get weaving, or you'll miss the Mess bus, and it's a five-mile walk!'

The Mess was an old chalk quarry, a smoky tunnel a hundred yards long and emerging straight into a coast road. The roof was pierced with ventilation shafts, but in the daytime there was insufficient current to work the fans; what there was of it was reserved for the dim bulbs and the water pumps. The air was heavy with the smell of sweat, cooking and tobacco smoke.

About a hundred and fifty NCOs from the fighter and torpedo-bomber squadrons slept and ate there all crowded together. The officers were no better off. Their billets had been bombed three times and they lived in a kind of gipsy encampment composed of tarpaulins and corrugated-iron sheets stretched over remains of walls. You roasted in summer and froze in winter. No one was worrying overmuch about the winter at this time as the question was rather whether Malta would hold out even till autumn.

Lunch consisted of five shrivelled olives, one slice of fried corned beef, four ounces of bread, three semi-ripe dried figs and a cup of tea. Pilots also had a right to two tablespoonfuls of raw shredded carrots soaked in cod-liver oil, for the essential vitamins, and a sulphur pill against diarrhoea.

Beurling was still too shaken by his eventful arrival to have any appetite. In addition, the pervading stink of petrol and oil smoke made his gorge rise. As there was no coal, the cookers were fed on old sump oil–a damaged aircraft was a godsend, as it meant hot soup for two or three days.

Poor Screwball! Scarcely six hours before, he had been getting outside a comfortable breakfast with all the

126

trimmings at a large waxed-oak table in the aircraft-carrier's air-conditioned mess–an absolute pleasure cruise! Now he was in a different world altogether. The fighter pilot's paradise! With all those Junkers 88s and Messerschmitt 109s spoiling for a fight it was possibly a paradise up in the air. But a paradise on earth, no!

He went and sat on a rickety chair with Hesslyn, a New Zealander, Buchanan, a South African, Gil Gilbert, Billy the Kid and a few others of his crowd. The contrast was striking between the clean-shaven unlined faces of the new arrivals from the *Eagle* in their new Gibraltar-issue battledress, and the stubbly faces–not a Gillette blade on the island–soiled shirts and tattered denims of the others.

'When Tedder passed this way a month ago,' said Mickey Butler, a Malta pilot of four months' standing who had already acquired seven confirmed successes, a DFM and dysentery, 'we shook him rigid; I thought he was going to get out his wallet and give us ten bob each to buy a new shirt!'

Knights of the Desert Air

Cecil Beaton, the famous photographer and designer, who was recruited by the Ministry of Information to record the progress of the war abroad, journeyed with the advancing forces into North Africa. One of the stops on his itinerary was with a Spitfire Squadron in the Libyan Desert in 1943, and these are his memories.

Once you have shown your passes and are admitted into the fraternity inside the barriers of the desert–yes, there is a barbed wire entrance to the desert–you will find a spirit comparable to that on a great ship many miles out at sea. Everyone isolated here is working together selflessly towards the same goal, each person is making his particular piece of effort towards the common cause, with no thought as to promotion or award. The result is most stimulating. In fact, in spite of everything, there is much to feel glad about in the desert.

To whichever service or allied nation he belongs, the stranger will find a welcome that is unimaginable else-where. He will be received without question, not only as an honoured guest, but as a long-lost friend. Everyone is a potential host; everyone seems jovial.

On my way to an air station, where they have Spitfires, we passed many large Prisoner of War camps, guarded by sentries perched high on lookout platforms. But these prisoners are mostly Italians and without any urge to escape. Their fate is to be kept penned up in this wasteland behind barbed wire, with little to pass away the days but the interest of three meals a day and a turn at the washing tap.

Another RAF Mess: I talked to several of the men here. They each have interesting stories to tell, if you can get them into the right mood and give them a feeling of friendliness. They enjoy an opportunity to talk to a newcomer. One of them confided, 'It's pretty foul, sometimes, when a bloke you have been with a lot doesn't come back. There was a chap named Jock that everyone liked especially. The day he "had it" the Commanding Officer was absolutely white in the face: "Jock didn't get back," was all he said, and he went off by himself. We felt particularly badly about it as Jock would have got a Bar to his DFC if he'd lived. And there was a fellow named Mac, a swell guy. I had a bad time of it when Mac "had it". He was a grand little chap, only about five feet tall but as brave as a lion–absolutely first class he was. I was the Flight Commander at the time, and we'd had a series of big "do's" over Benghazi. Mac had been out on the previous show, a terrific one, but he begged me to let him go again this time. He was a wizard pilot, had just been made a Pilot Officer, and his enthusiasm was terrific. Well, I let him go. That night the ack-ack was brutal. Buckets of it everywhere. The aircraft were lurching about in a regular fifth of November firework display. It's not funny having to "deliver the groceries" in those circumstances. With shells bursting near the side of the plane, any moment, I thought I would have "had it". Suddenly I saw someone alongside me "had it". There was a terrific explosion which knocked me end over tip and then I saw that one of our bombers had been hit. It looked like a blazing waterfall, bits falling everywhere. It was terrific. When we got back I found out it was Mac who had got that shell. I've never felt so badly about anything before. But the funny thing about it was that some months later we were in the mess, when there, at the other end of the tent, in a Captain's uniform, was the very living image of Mac–I could hardly believe my eyes. I really thought I was seeing things. It made me feel quite ropy. The CO came over quietly and said he wanted me to talk to this chap. He was the exact replica of Mac, only wearing glasses and a bit greyer, perhaps even thinner and smaller. We had a drink together, he said he was a Captain in the last war, and talked about nothing in particular, when suddenly he asked if we couldn't go somewhere where it was quiet and he could talk to me alone. "Mac often mentioned you in his letters: Mac was my only son," he said, "Mac was all I cared about in the world, all I had to live for, in fact. My wife had died, my daughter was killed in the bombing at Birmingham and, as you know, Mac has gone. Now I want you to tell me exactly how he met his death. I don't want to be spared anything. I don't want you to think of my feelings, but I'm haunted by the idea of not knowing what happened to him. You must tell me everything."

'"But, Sir, I can't do that, we never do."

'"But I insist, I want you to tell me exactly what happened, I must know."

'"But, Sir, in the Service that's one thing we never talk about, it's just one of those unwritten rules that aren't broken."

'"I insist!", the little man said emphatically, beating his fist on his knee, "I told the Commanding Officer that was my intention in wanting to speak to you."

'Well, you can imagine how embarrassed I felt. I called for a double whiskey each, and then another and yet another. After a time we were both well "under way", but I could "take" it better than he could and I gave him more than I took. I started to tell him some stories and he told me some. We roared with laughter, and we had quite a jolly evening until eventually he passed out completely. Two of our fellows had to carry him off and we gave him a bed for the night.

'Poor little chap, it was not at all a "good show" really, and I felt rather badly about what I had done. But what else could I do? I mean it wasn't any good getting morbid, he would only have cried or done something stupid like that.'

Another evening a young Flight Lieutenant from Liverpool, with heavy eyebrows and a great smile, told me how he had been asked to shoot his line. 'Shoot your line, mm–how?' I said. He explained:

'We were quite pleased with ourselves. The Squadron had got a bag of six in two days. We were having a celebration in the mess when Patterson, the orderly, said I was wanted on the telephone.

"We want you to talk on the BBC," some darned voice drawled at me.

'I thought it was a gag, told the blighter what I thought of him and hung up.

'"Some nut trying to pull my leg," I told the others. They all laughed–"Oh, that's grand, old Beany shooting a line over the air, that'd be first class! Intrepid Birdman! Oh, first class! Ha! Ha!"

'Next morning the bloke called me again–said it was on the level, they wanted me to come to Cairo to talk on the radio. The CO had given his OK. I telephoned the CO and told him some ruddy fool was trying to make an ass of me; what did he know about it? Suddenly he gave me a hell of a rocket: "You damned well do as you're told, it's an order; don't ask me stupid questions and get cracking without wasting more time."

'Well, I didn't mind the idea of having a "shufti" in Cairo, not that I like Cairo any, but it's good to get a bath and an ice-cold drink. Well, I arrived at the BBC place feeling rather a fool.

'"Have you had time to write anything?" a bloke asked me.

'"Write anything, me write? I've never written anything in my life."

'"Well, you were on that daylight sweep over Martuba, weren't you?–we want you to broadcast to London about it tonight on the nine o'clock news. Well now, you just make some notes, saying what happened, quite straight-forward. People want to know what it feels like, you know. It was a jolly good show."

'"That's a hell of an order to give a chap in cold blood," I said, "got anything to steady me?"

'"Why, sure." He produced some whiskey, a bottle of it, damned good stuff too, and it helped a lot. I put down a few notes, but there isn't much to say, is there? What's the point of pretending the bombs, dropped by the bombers we were escorting, looked like bursting oranges, or balls of fire, or any sort of balls, or that the Me 109s fell out of the sky like confetti. Anyhow, when I had done what I could the bloke said it was not exciting enough. You haven't told us anything, he said.

'So we had to go over it together. He asked me a lot of damn-fool questions, and I said "Yes" to almost every-thing. After a terrific sweat we concocted some terrific line-shooting tripe, ending up "It certainly was just a piece of cake."

'"Have it your own way," I said. 'The bloke smiled, "Now you go off and come back at three o'clock and we'll make a record of it."

'"Almighty!" The thought of that didn't make me feel too good. Oh, what the hell! I went off and had a damned good lunch and I felt swell and forgot all about the broadcast. It was wizard being in a nice cool hotel with lots of women about.

'It's quite a change having a "shufti" around Cairo after the desert.

'Well, somehow or other it was 4.30 when I got back to

the BBC. The bloke had a look at me, and said, "Had a good lunch, eh? Well, you'd better rehearse the thing first, hadn't you?"

'"Rehearse nothing, shoot!"

'Well, the first time I did it fine, except I gave a hiccough in the middle of a word. At the second crack I didn't hiccough, but somehow or other I read the same sentence twice running. Would you believe it, I had to do the damn thing four times! I was completely "brassed off" with the whole damned thing, but when it was over the bloke gave me another drink, and then just one more to finish the bottle.

'The chaps made a hell of a noise when they heard me shooting my line on the mess radio. It wasn't too bad, though, really. They don't pay you anything of course, but still I got a free bottle of whiskey out of it.'

Chasing the Flying Bombs

Sqaudron Leader Tom Berry was one of the Spitfire pilots who remained in Britain throughout the war, and played a crucial role in the defence of London when the Germans attempted a final 80-day bombardment with their new robot Flying Bombs in the summer of 1944. In all, fighter pilots shot down 1,900 of these missiles–Squadron Leader Berry accounting for some 60 of these before his death in action. The following extract is from a radio broadcast he made that same summer.

There is a new kind of battle going on in the skies over London–Spitfires versus the German Flying Bombs. These deadly missiles which have been nicknamed 'Doodle Bugs' are another attempt by Hitler to try to bring this nation to its knees. But, just as happened in the Battle of Britain, I believe our fighters will prove to be too good, and in fact we've already knocked a thousand of them out of the skies before they have been able to inflict any damage on the capital city.

There are lots of stories being told about the bravery of the pilots in tackling these Flying Bombs. Only the other day I saw an old Cockney sorting through the rubble of what had once been his home–hit by one of the bombs–and yet he could still look upwards as a plane flew overhead and smile, 'It's them young fellas in those Spitfires wot are savin' London!'

And recently I heard a report from the South of England about a chase between three Spitfires and a 'Doodle Bug'. Apparently it was heading in over the coast in the direction of an anti-aircraft battery, but the planes were so close the gunners were afraid of opening up in case they hit one of chaps.

The men and women of the gun-site heard the fighters' guns and then saw the bomb begin to falter. Horrified, they saw it was going to plunge right onto *them*–and yet still they could do nothing.

But at this precise moment, one of the Spitfires raced level with the now erratic missile, and 'formating' and 'flipping' it with a wing tip, turned it off course. The bomb crashed about 250 yards from the gun position and well clear of any houses. Did everyone sigh with relief!

I have also been interested to learn that when the Germans were trying out their prototype Flying Bombs, they tested them for speed against a captured Spitfire flown by a Luftwaffe pilot. It seems Hitler watched this test and was very impressed with the missile's performance.

What the Germans didn't know was that the Spitfire was an old Mark V model, inferior in speed to the subsequent Spitfires, and so their belief that the missile could outrun any British fighter was incorrect right from the word go!

Mind you, I can say from personal experience that the 'Doodle Bug' doesn't go down easily. It will take a lot of punishment, and you have to aim at the propulsion unit– that's the long stove-pipe, as we call it, on the tail.

If your range and aim are dead on, you can see pieces flying off the stove-pipe. The big white flame at the end goes out, and down goes the bomb.

Sometimes it dives straight to earth, but at other times it goes crazy and gives a wizard display of aerobatics before finally crashing. Sometimes the bomb explodes in mid-air, and the flash is so blinding that you cannot see a thing for about ten seconds.

If this happens, you hope to be the right way up when you are able to see again, because the explosion often throws the fighter about and sometimes even turns it upside down!

Dicing with Death

Air Commodore Howard Williams describes another function which the Spitfire performed with great flexibility–aerial reconnaissance over Europe. The pilots of these planes were dubbed 'The Highest Flyers in the World', and they themselves referred to their vital but dangerous missions as 'Dicing With Death'.

The men who flew in the RAF home-based Photographic Reconnaissance squadrons, whose area of operations extended from the north of Norway to Gibraltar, were known among their fellows as 'The Highest Flyers in the World'.

These pilots, who flew in the sub-stratosphere all over Europe on behalf of their own Service as well as the Navy, the Army and the Ministry of Economic Warfare, used special Spitfires for their missions.

For their safety, they relied on great height, high speed and routing. The fact that they had a vastly better plane than the enemy–and knew it–was largely the reason for their success, although much also depended on the pilots' own abilities and resources.

The men, mostly volunteers, were first tested in a pressure chamber on the ground to ensure that they could stand the strains imposed. Oxygen bottles were used in flights as the Spitfires were not equipped with a pressurised cabin.

The cameras which the planes first carried secured a very small likeness at 30,000 feet. Indeed, they showed 40 square miles of country to a scale of 1 in 80,000, on a negative 5 inches square.

Cameras with longer focal lengths presented their problems, however. They would not fit into the wings, and had to go into the fuselage. But eventually all the difficulties were overcome.

In 1943, when the missions were really running smoothly, the Spitfires were equipped with twin cameras of 14.20 and 36 inch focal length, which precisely covered a few miles of territory despite the heights at which they were operated. Worked by remote control electrically from the cockpit, they could take up to 500 pictures.

Within an hour or two of the pilot's landing, the prints were ready. A full report of the film would follow in two days, and by matching the photographs taken in sequence it was possible to obtain a stereoscopic picture of the territory.

As viewed from films taken by sub-stratosphere planes, the bomb damage to London looked as if it had been done with a screwdriver, while that to places like Hamburg, Remscheid and Wuppertal looked as if a steamroller had been used!

Not all the photography that these intrepid Spitfire pilots carried out was sub-stratosphere work. Sometimes it was necessary for them to go in low over certain territory through a mass of anti-aircraft fire. This became known colloquially among the men as 'Dicing', its origin being that well-known phrase, 'Dicing with Death'!

A Bird's-Eye View of Destruction

Richard Dimbleby, the BBC's first war correspondent, visited every theatre of war in 14 different countries to relay news of the conflict back to the millions of listeners in Britain and Europe. As the Nazi empire began to crumble, he flew on bombing raids over Germany, and later was to become the first English correspondent to enter Berlin when the German capital fell in May, 1945. In the following vivid account he describes a mission over Germany in late 1944 and reveals–most appropriately–how the Spitfire which had first stood up to the might of Hitler was now dominating the skies as the Führer's mad dream was at last being laid into dust and rubble.

14 October 1944

I think that not only in the smoke and rubble of Duisburg, but deeper in the heart of Germany, there must be men charged with the defence of the Reich whose hearts tonight are filled with dread and despair. For the unbelievable thing has come to pass–the RAF has delivered its greatest single attack against a German industrial target since the start of the war–more than a thousand heavy bombers, more than 4,500 tons of bombs– and it did it, this morning, in broad daylight.

At a quarter to nine this morning I was over the Rhine and Duisburg in a Lancaster, one of the thousand and more four-engined machines that filled the sunny sky to the north and south and east. A year ago it would have been near suicide to appear over the Ruhr in daylight–a trip by night was something to remember uncomfortably for a long time. Today, as the great broad stream of Lancasters and Halifaxes crossed the frontier of Germany, there was not an aircraft of the Luftwaffe to be seen in the sky, only the twisting and criss-crossing vapour trails of our own Spitfires and Mustangs protecting us far above and on the flanks.

The briefing officer had described Duisburg as the largest inland port in the world and an arsenal of the Reich when he addressed the air crews. I saw Duisburg the arsenal, just for a moment, in a hole in the patchy white clouds that lay over the Rhine and the Ruhr. I saw the grey patchwork of houses and factories, roads, railways, and the dirty dark waters of the great river curving its way through the inland port. Then target indicators and bombs, HE and incendiary, nearly 5,000 tons of them, went shooting down; and the German flak, and a good deal of it, came shooting up. Duisburg the arsenal disappeared under a filthy billowing brown bulge of smoke. I saw no fires from our Lancaster–there was too much cloud for that–and I had one nervous eye on the chessboard of black bursting shells that had been super-imposed on our fine clear piece of sky. But I *did* see heavy bombs, cookies, going down into the brown smoke, and more clouds of it pushing their sullen way up from the ground. Duisburg lay underneath the shroud; and shroud, I think, is the right word.

In case it sounds rather easy, this smashing of German targets by day, let me say at once that the pilots who are going to do it from now on are taking very great risks each time they set out on such an operation. The best they can hope for is a thick curtain of bursting shells through which to fly, and the sight–the sight that we had this morning– of one or two of their companions twisting down to the ground in flames and smoke. But such hazards do not affect the plans of Bomber Command, that astonishingly versatile organisation that began the war with so little and by courage and perseverance has built up today's striking force. As we flew home this morning and saw a tight orderly patch of Flying Fortresses engaged on their Cologne operation passing us above the clouds, I could not help but realise that, together, Britain and America can now put into the morning or afternoon sky a mighty force of bombers that spells destruction and ruin for our enemies.

The Shotgun Plane

Alexander McKee, one of the leading modern historians and author of the classic account of Britain's air war, *Strike from the Sky* (1960), here summarises the various opinions of the Spitfire which he has collected from those most closely involved, and draws a conclusion with which there can surely be no argument.

The late C. G. Grey of *The Aeroplane* used to say that if an aircraft looked right, it was right. By this test, the Spitfire was classically perfect. The lines were as aesthetically beautiful as those of a Greek or Etruscan statue.

That the Spitfire was as effective as it was lovely became clear without doubt when I came to interview British and German pilots for my book on the Battle of Britain, *Strike from the Sky*. One question I put to them all was, how did the Spitfire and Hurricane compare with the Messerschmitt 109?

From their replies I concluded that the 109 had one marked advantage over both British fighters, in that its direct-injection engine enabled it to nose over into a dive and simply drop away from them; neither Spitfire nor Hurricane could follow until their float-type carburettors had been modified. The 109 had a higher ceiling than the Spitfire I but the Spitfire II, equipped with the Rotol constant-speed propeller, had a markedly improved rate of climb, ceiling, and manœuvrability at height.

Johannes Steinhof, a leading German fighter pilot, and later a Brigade General in the post-war Luftwaffe, told me, 'At the start the 109 had a certain advantage, except for its turning radius, but the later Spitfire had a higher ceiling and better climb.'

Adolf Galland summed up for me: 'The Spitfire was dangerous, on account of its armament, climb, manœuvrability, and the courage of its pilots. Mölders and Udet favoured a concentration of armament in the nose of the aircraft. That's a good idea for a very good shot. But the average pilot is not so good, he needs something like a shotgun. And the Spitfire was a real shotgun. So, when it was fighter versus fighter, even if you tried to shoot the enemy down while turning, the Spitfire was better.'

Jeffrey Quill, Spitfire test-pilot who fought in the Battle of Britain, said, 'It was certainly necessary to pull out all the stops in order to fight the 109s, but at altitude we had the edge on them and they treated the Spitfire with respect.'

Both Steinhof and Galland had smiled when the Hurricane was mentioned. 'The Hurricane was a big disadvantage to you, the rate of roll being bad–we were lucky to meet Hurricanes,' commented Steinhof. 'The Hurricane was hopeless–a nice aeroplane to shoot down,' said Galland.

M. V. Blake, who flew both types, said, 'The Spit was an infinitely superior aircraft, although I loved the Hurricane. The Spit was like a fine blade cutting through the air–a precision instrument; it and the 109 were so close that the chap who had the height advantage would be the victor.'

Al Deere, a New Zealander who flew Spitfire IIs with 54 Squadron, summed up: 'The Hurricane and the Spitfire were complementary. The Hurricane was the better gun platform and therefore more effective against bombers, but it could not have lived without Spitfires to take on the

109s, whereas the Spitfires could have lived without the Hurricanes.'

The public image of the Spitfire as the legendary victor of 1940 seems near enough true.

The Legend Flies On

Such, indeed, were the qualities of the Spitfire that it remained in front-line service with the RAF for another six years after the end of the Second World War. In fact, it was not until 1948 that the last model, the F24, came off the production line. Just 81 of these were built, all being modified versions of the earlier F22 and powered by 2,035 hp Griffon 61 engines. The very last of these brought the grand total of Spitfires manufactured in the ten years since the advent of the Mark IA to a huge 20,351. (Just to complete the record, I should add that another 2,408 Seafires, the 'navalised' carrier version of the Spitfire for the Fleet Air Arm, were built between 1941 and 1949; as well as 373 Spitefuls, another four-cannon variation which served with the RAF until made obsolete by the arrival of jet fighters.)

The last of this great line, the Mark F24 was, without doubt, the Spitfire in its most perfect form as an interceptor fighter. It is arguable whether anything further could have been done to improve its performance, manœuvrability and strike power. Yet when the last 24 of these F24s were mothballed in 1952 (later, tragically, to be scrapped!) it seemed as if Mitchell's magnificent aeroplane would soon be no more than just a footnote in history.

But, in truth, a legend was already growing. Although R. J. Mitchell was the most private of men, memorials to him proliferated. The Schneider Trophy and one of his S6 seaplanes which represented his pioneering work were put on permanent display in the Science Museum in London. A Junior High School at Hornchurch, from where the Spitfire had flown during the Battle of Britain, was named after him, as was a Youth Centre in his birthplace at Hanley, Stoke-on-Trent. And most of all, of course, a true appreciation of the worth of the Spitfire began to grow, resulting in beautifully preserved examples being put on display not only in this country, but also in many places abroad where the valiant fighter had helped win the great battle for freedom.

Back in the late 1940s it was the pilots who had flown the Spitfire who were the saddest to see it go. It was perhaps only right, though, that when the first jet fighter was developed in Britain, a Spitfire squadron should be the first to be re-equipped with this new plane. It was the twin-engined Gloster Meteor, soon to prove the heir to the Spitfire's role as the RAF's premier interceptor.

A great deal of secrecy surrounded the development of this Rolls Royce-engined plane, the creation of Air Commodore Frank Whittle. Special precautions were taken from the days when the very first prototype flew in May, 1941, and thereafter no flights were permitted over enemy territory in case one should fall into German hands. The effectiveness and potential of the Meteor were brilliantly underlined when one intercepted and shot down a Flying Bomb on August 4, 1944.

One of the first former Spitfire pilots to fly the Meteor was Flight Lieutenant David Morris and in February, 1945, he gave these impressions of the new fighter. 'They are really beautiful aircraft,' he said. 'When they start up and taxi out the "squirts" [engines] make a noise rather like an oversized vacuum cleaner. But when they take off, or fly at full throttle, they sound like a normal aircraft.

The "squirts" have plenty of power, too–they go up like a lift. There is also plenty of armour to give one a sense of security, and the cockpit layout differs very little from the conventional type.'

It was typical of a Spitfire man, honed by the exacting demands of war, to take to this revolutionary new form of aircraft in such confident style.

The general public would not easily forget the Spitfire, either, although it was to be some years before surviving models were put into position on airfields and in museums for all to admire. As well as those listed in the final section of this book, 'Spitfires on Show', there are a substantial number more in private hands and others on display in places like Paris, Brussels, Eindhoven, Copenhagen, Ottawa, Athens, Rangoon, Thailand, Singapore, Johannesburg, Canberra and Auckland.

The legend of the plane has also been substantiated in a plethora of books about the war–the Battle of Britain in particular–as well as in a number of films. The Spitfire, in fact, enjoys the distinction unique among aircraft of being the subject of a movie about its creation, *The First of the Few*, made in 1942. This picture was not only a great success at the box office, but also an accurate and authentic recreation of the events that took place: a distinction very few war films can claim! It was also notable for a musical score by Sir William Walton, *Spitfire Prelude and Fugue*, still looked upon today as one of the most moving pieces by this composer.

The First of the Few told the story of R. J. Mitchell and his creation of the Spitfire, spanning 20 years from the days of his early triumphs in the Schneider Trophy races to the full-flowering of his genius in the Battle of Britain. The picture was very much the idea of its star, Leslie Howard, who not only took the title role, but was also the producer and director.

Howard had heard about Mitchell during the Battle of Britain and by the following year was fired up with the

147

idea of making a picture about him. 'The story has a great appeal at this stage of the war,' he told his wife Doodie as they discussed the project in 1941. 'After all, the Spitfire saved us in the Battle of Britain, and this man giving his own life was really the same as "The Few" who were killed flying the plane. He was, in fact, the very first of "The Few".'

To co-star in the picture, Howard recruited the talented David Niven to play an ex-RAF pilot who tested Mitchell's prototypes–a singularly unlikely casting on the face of it, for Niven had to be given leave from his post in the Army to appear! Nevertheless, he was splendid in the part.

The First of the Few captured Mitchell's private battle with cancer as well as his public war with authority to see his dream through to completion. It also authentically recreated the Battle of Britain scenes, with location shooting at Ibsley Aerodrome near Ringwood in Hampshire; and as the war was, of course, still continuing, many of the flying shots were filmed on dispersal in actual battle conditions. Various of the supporting roles were performed by pilots stationed at Ibsley, led by their Squadron Leader Frankie Howell, DFC and Bar.

After the war, the Squadron's former intelligence officer, G. A. Le Mesurier, recalled how the picture had been made. 'Leslie Howard and David Niven spent months with the Squadron while we were on active operations. They spared no pains in producing an authentic story under genuine war conditions, even down to having the script vetted by the pilots to ensure the use of the jargon common among them.

'It was part of my job to obtain reports from the pilots when they landed from operational sorties. This proved no sinecure because immediately on landing the pilots would tear off the set hotly pursued by a perspiring and portly IO intent on getting the gen before they had forgotten all in the excitement of being embryo film stars!

The result, though, was an epic.'

The critics shared the opinion that the picture was an epic. The doyenne of reviewers, Dilys Powell of *The Sunday Times*, wrote that *The First of the Few* was 'well and excitingly told, with a careful balancing of professional and domestic incident. It is the story of a man to whom we owe a great debt, our lives, perhaps, told in a form which ensures public attention.'

In America, where the movie was retitled *Spitfire*, the weekly magazine *Time* was equally enthusiastic and called it, 'a finely tasteful, faithful biography of one of Britain's least known heroes . . . for as the designer of the tactically superior Spitfire fighter, Mitchell was one of the few men–Churchill was another–whose foresight had much to do with saving Britain and her allies. The picture also contains some hair-raising shots of the kind of Spitfire action that the designer sadly never saw.

'*Spitfire* is in no way a slick, machine-turned production; it has, on the contrary, a virtue uncommon in contemporary films–the look and texture of the lovingly handmade article. It has also the quiet discretion that always distinguished Leslie Howard as an actor,' the magazine added.

Tragically, *The First of the Few* also served as Leslie Howard's epitaph, for the following year, just three hours after attending a première of the picture in Lisbon on June 14, the unarmed Dutch KLM DC3 civil airliner in which he was travelling back to London was shot down over the Bay of Biscay by German Ju 88 bombers. The mystery as to whether this was deliberately planned by the Nazis because of Howard's successful propaganda activities in Spain and Portugal–or because there was a man on the flight with a distinct resemblance to Churchill (actually Howard's manager, Alfred Chenhalls)–has never been solved. Whatever the case, it was a murderous end to the career of a fine actor who had also played a significant part in expanding the legend of the Spitfire on

149

the cinema screen.

Curiously, however, *The First of the Few* was not the first picture to have featured a Spitfire. A year earlier, in 1941, American director Henry King had made *A Yank in the RAF* with Tyrone Power starring as an American who joins a Spitfire squadron and takes part in the evacuation of Dunkirk. Betty Grable, the famous 'Forces' Pin-Up', co-starred with Power in a story which made rather more of the US contribution to the dramatic rescue operation than had, in fact, occurred! That same year, Ronald Reagan, the B-movie actor destined to become President of the United States, turned up as a bomber pilot ferrying planes to England in *International Squadron*. In a role owing something to Errol Flynn, he helped out a British fighter squadron short on pilots by taking part in a Spitfire mission as if he had been flying the planes all his life!

Eagle Squadron, which Universal Pictures released in 1942, was dedicated to the small group of intrepid young American pilots who had crossed the Atlantic to fight in the Battle of Britain. Directed by Arthur Lubin, it was introduced by war correspondent Quentin Reynolds, and starred Robert Stack, Jon Hall, Eddie Albert and Leif Erikson as the Eagles in a squadron commanded by Nigel Bruce. Based on a story by C. S. Forester, the picture was highlighted by some fine semi-documentary sequences of Spitfire sweeps over France. Dilys Powell once again enjoyed this kind of action and commented, '*Eagle Squadron* is greatly assisted by the fact that Hollywood, unlike, say Denham, is enabled when it makes a flying film to present the warplanes in the plural and not merely the singular or the dual.' This said, the movie actually only featured *three* Spitfires!

The veteran movie maker, Raoul Walsh, had rather more of the planes at his disposal when he made *Fighter Squadron* some three years after the end of the war: although he had to go to considerable expense to find and restore examples which he was then at liberty to crash! His excellent camera technique produced some fine low shots of the fighters in action, as the stills from the picture vividly illustrate.

Angels One Five, which Associated British-Pathe released in 1952, returned once more to the theme of the Battle of Britain, but Hurricanes were the stars of this story. The plot concerned the 'Pimpernel' squadron and the conflicts which can exist not only between a pilot and his enemy, but also with others on the same side. Jack Hawkins and Michael Denison starred in the picture based on a story by Wing Commander A. J. C. Pelham Groom who also served as Technical Adviser. As a point of interest, director George More O'Ferrall found Hurricanes so hard to come by he had to borrow a group of them belonging to the Portuguese Government!

Malta Story, another British production from Rank Studios the following year, brought back Jack Hawkins to the screen along with Alec Guinness and Anthony Steele in an excellent reconstruction of that brave island's heroic resistance to the Germans. Though much of the drama was concentrated on the local population and their defiance of the bombing raids, the arrival of the Spitfires on Malta and their subsequent crucial role in keeping the enemy at bay was dramatically staged and photographed. The production team also cleverly managed to make just three operational Spitfires look like dozens!

The story of Sir Douglas Bader which was told in *Reach For The Sky* (1956) was every bit as critically well-received as had been Paul Brickhill's biography on which it was based. Kenneth Moore played the heroic Bader with consummate skill and a nice touch of humour, and managed to convey the airman's all-pervasive tenacity of purpose in a way that earned even the subject's praise. The climactic sequence showing the dramatic fly-over of London by 300 aircraft on September 15, 1945, when Bader led the formation in a Battle of Britain Spitfire, proved just as dramatic on the screen as it had done on the actual day of that great celebration.

Though Wing Commander Bader (as he then was) came down to watch the filming of some of the location shooting at Kenley RAF Station, he refused point blank to attend the London première of the film on July 5, 1956. Instead he was found playing golf in Scotland and commented with typical modesty, 'I am very flattered and I think it is very wonderful they should have made a film of my life. And people have said some very nice things. But I am not a blooming film star! I couldn't go along to a première having my photograph taken with a lot of celebrities, then thinking to myself, "Look–that's you up on the screen. You're a hero." It's different seeing it with a crowd of the boys when you can have a good laugh if you want to!'

Bader did, though, think the picture directed by Lewis Gilbert was excellent–'although they could hardly be expected to get everything right,' he said. It was in fact later named the Best British Film of 1956.

Another British aeronautical institution, Cranwell, was featured in *High Flight* (1957) with Ray Milland and Kenneth Haigh in a story of intrigue among young trainee pilots.

The most recent film to feature the Spitfire extensively was, of course, Harry Saltzman's epic *Battle of Britain* (1969), with its huge cast of stars including Michael Caine and Robert Shaw as RAF Squadron Leaders, Nigel Patrick as a Group Captain, Trevor Howard playing Air Vice Marshal Keith Park, Patrick Wymark as Air Vice Marshal Trafford Leigh-Mallory, and Laurence Olivier as Air Chief Marshal Sir Hugh Dowding. (Kenneth Moore was also in the line-up as a Group Captain Baker!) With a screenplay by James Kennaway and Wilfred Greatorex, the picture was directed for Saltzman's appropriately named Spitfire Productions by Guy Hamilton.

However, despite this roster of some of Britain's finest

actors, it was the aircraft which undoubtedly stole the picture. And it was very much thanks to the dogged research of one man that such an impressive array of wartime machines appeared before the cameras. He was Group Captain Hamish Mahaddie, a former wartime Pathfinder, who spent three and a half years tracking down both British and German aircraft.

'It all began in Hyde Park when the associate producer, Benjamin Fisz, and I saw a lone Spitfire performing a victory roll during a rehearsal for a Royal fly-past,' the former 'Bomber Baron', as Mahaddie likes to call himself, explains. 'Benny wondered just how many Spitfires were left in the world, and we guessed maybe four or five. But the thought kept nagging at the back of my mind and so I began to check. By the end of the week I had tracked down 100.'

This discovery gave the incentive to the producers to make a new version of the Battle of Britain story, utilising all the special camera techniques now available. Mahaddie set off on his 'search and find' mission, and as a result of travelling twice around the world and spending over £100,000 on acquisitions, could report back to his friend, 'I believe there are around 200 Spitfires still in existence in the world. And I have personally touched or seen 116.'

Group Captain Mahaddie found Hurricanes the hardest of British aircraft to come by–he could only locate eight–and the German Messerschmitts and Heinkel bombers almost impossible. But gradually his 'air force' was assembled, and then for several summer months in 1968 the most famous aerial battle of the war was refought for the cameras over southern England and the English Channel. To ensure authenticity, several of the leading figures in the battle were recruited to observe the filming, and there were nostalgic reunions for the likes of Lord Dowding, Wing Commander Bader, Group Captain Brian Kingcome and even Major General Adolf Galland.

The event caused Lord Dowding to reminisce with a

smile, 'They were a wonderful set of fellows, my pilots. I don't think there has ever been anything quite like the same light-heartedness and spirit in the face of an issue that was anything but light-hearted. Yet we were all alive to the fact that it was a deadly game. But I felt instinctively with these fellows I gathered around me that, whatever happened, they wouldn't let me down. I don't think they were just a unique generation–they were the last of a breed!'

All told, though, the Spitfires were the real stars of the film, and the very fact that there were still so many around provided a real incentive to the small but ever-expanding group of enthusiasts who were dedicated to finding and restoring the aircraft.

Today this business of restoration goes on with increasing intensity, and Spitfires in all their glory are re-emerging from the most unlikely-looking wrecks and piles of spare parts. Some have been unearthed from the fields where they crashed, others from the bottom of lakes, and some even reassembled from the most fragmented parts collected from places all over the world where the plane once served. In Britain alone, Spitfire rebuilds are becoming almost commonplace, and as I write five are under way, with two machines on the verge of flying once again.

Perhaps one of the most remarkable discoveries of recent years occurred in the summer of 1982 when, following a five-year search, a group of enthusiasts in Scotland located and raised Spitfire P7540 which had lain in the murky waters of Loch Doon in the Galloway Hills for over 40 years. The plane, from 312 Squadron, had plunged into the lake while on a training flight from RAF Ayr in October, 1941. Fortunately a water bailiff had seen the crash, and though the RAF gave up the search after only a short while in 1941, when the enthusiasts turned up years later in 1977, he was able to help them succeed.

The wreckage was found to be scattered under the loch

for a distance of almost 200 metres, but piece by piece, from a section of the rear fuselage and tail section to the actual Merlin XII engine, the Spitfire was reclaimed by divers from its watery grave, until virtually 90 per cent had been recovered. These sections were found to be in remarkably good condition with little major corrosion, and they are now being painstakingly reassembled at the local Aviation Museum on the former airfield at Tinwald Downs. The find represents yet another important piece in the jigsaw of Spitfire history.

The actual business of a Spitfire 'rebuild' is, of course, an immensely complicated one, and would require far more space than could easily be justified in a general study of the aeroplane such as this one. But information is available on some of the more recent reconstructions, in the form of leaflets, while there have been a number of articles in aeronautical journals about some of the individuals who are gaining recognition for their skill in restoring the shattered remains of Spitfires into fully operational machines.

One of the most enterprising members of this group is 36 year-old Steve Atkins of Sussex, who can trace his fascination with the Spitfire back to a very precise moment in time. He was out on his bicycle one summer day in 1968.

'I was nineteen at the time,' he recalls, 'and they were filming *Battle of Britain* over the south coast. The camera plane went overhead followed by six Spitfires. The look and sound of them stunned me. I didn't go back to work for a fortnight: I just followed those aircraft around.'

This incredible experience for a young man who had not even been born when the Spitfire had passed its heyday, immediately inspired him to learn to fly. But he soon knew he would never actually get to pilot a Spitfire unless he owned one himself. After months of searching he finally found a battered model in Scotland and promptly swapped it for his own light plane *and* a substantial amount of money. Steve's friends thought he was mad–he readily admits today–but he believed this would be the key to satisfying his obsession with the plane. While restoring *his* Spitfire, he would do the same thing for other rich collectors not possessed of his mechanical skill.

'A wartime Spitfire cost about £5,000, and in 1946 their scrap value was £100,' Steve says. 'But when I have finished restoration, the sale price is about £275,000. Now that's not a bargain price, but a realistic one. The money may strike people as ridiculous, but the fact is that there are far more people in the world willing to invest on that scale than there are flying Spitfires to satisfy the demand.'

There is plenty of evidence to support his claim, too. In August, 1984, for instance, a Spitfire Mark II reconnaissance model, PR XI PL983, was put up for auction at Duxford Airfield, and although the bidding reached £320,000 this was £30,000 *below* the reserve price which the owner, a former French pilot in the RAF, Roland Fraissinet, had put on his pride and joy. And after passing up this small fortune, M. Fraissinet was quite happy to admit, 'You see, I fell in love with the Spitfire all over again when I first got it. I could not be more delighted that it was not sold!'

Steve Atkins fully understands the mystique which the aeroplane exerts on its admirers. 'Without doubt,' he says, 'it is the most beautiful aircraft ever built. Viewed from any angle it's all graceful curves–it looks good, exactly *right*. It's a classic, a thoroughbred; there is nothing else like it.'

However, he confesses that the plane is a 'swine' to rebuild. 'Reginald Mitchell was a genius and a very stubborn man,' he explains. 'The Spitfire must have been a nightmare to mass-produce because, really, it has to be handbuilt. Spare parts are a problem. Enthusiasts have them hoarded away, but they won't sell, they want to swop.'

Steve plans to sell flights in his own Spitfire, a rare kind of two-seater trainer, at about £600 an hour. Again this figure is not difficult to justify. The engine rebuild cost £16,000 (including 500 hours of work), the insurance is £17,000, and the aircraft uses a gallon of fuel per minute, at £2.50 per gallon.

'But there is no shortage of bookings,' he says. 'When Spitfires fly past at displays many onlookers cry. And they all dream of actually flying in one.'

And as more and more old Spitfires are located and made operational again, so they become more in evidence at air displays, fly-ins, air shows, open days at RAF stations, and marvellous annual spectacles such as the 'Great Warbirds Show' at West Malling, Kent, and the 'Fighter Meets' at the old Battle of Britain base at North Weald in Essex.

All this is evidence of just how widely the interest in the Spitfire is growing year by year. And among those who can never hope to own an actual plane, the quest for memorabilia grows more determined–and more profitable. At auctions items of equipment from the plane, or from the pilots who flew them, will fetch hundreds of pounds, and even authentic models of the plane will attract bids in the region of £250. The sheepskin jackets worn by Spitfire pilots rarely go for less than £150.

This public enthusiasm is very heartwarming to people like ex-RAF pilot Group Captain David Green, the founder of The Spitfire Society of Great Britain. He is pleased at everything that is going towards preserving the legend of the great fighter plane.

'A lot of enthusiasts are putting a lot of hard work into rebuilding planes which have been found in the most dreadful state,' he says. 'But I'm not sure it will be the same with modern aircraft. Today's jet jockeys are not as careful with the machines as we used to be!

'I think it's unlikely now that there will ever be such a thing as the "last Spitfire",' Group Captain Green adds with real satisfaction in his voice.*

And should you glance up into our summer skies when any air display is taking place, I am sure you will see the evidence to justify his words. R. J. Mitchell's magnificent creation surely well deserves to be still flying 50 years after its birth.

*Interestingly, The Spitfire Society is building an exact replica of the prototype Spitfire K5054 to mark the plane's 50th anniversary and to be put on permanent exhibition, probably in the RAF Museum at Hendon in a proposed Spitfire Hall.

Spitfires on Show

Hereunder are listed the Spitfires which are most readily accessible for viewing by members of the public. The location of each plane is given first, then its serial number, date of manufacture, and the Squadron or Unit to which it was first delivered.

MARK I
Battle of Britain Museum, Hendon. X4590. Built 1940. No. 609 Squadron, Middle Wallop.
Imperial War Museum, London. R6915. Built 1940. No. 609 Squadron, Middle Wallop.
RAF Museum, Hendon. K9942. Built 1939. No. 72 Squadron, Church Fenton.
Science Museum, London. P9444. Built 1940. No. 72 Squadron, Church Fenton.

MARK II
Dumfries and Galloway Aviation Museum, Scotland. P7540. Built 1939. No. 312 Squadron, RAF Ayr.
RAF Battle of Britain Memorial Flight, Coningsby. P7350. Built 1938. No. 266 (Rhodesia) Squadron, Wittering.

MARK V
Manchester Air and Space Museum. BL614. Built 1941. No. 611 Squadron (AAF), Drem.
RAF Battle of Britain Memorial Flight, Coningsby. AB910. Built 1941. No. 222 Squadron, North Weald.
RAF Linton upon Ouse, Yorkshire. BM597. Built 1942. No. 315 Squadron, Burtonwood.
RAF Wattisham, Suffolk. EP120. Built 1942. No. 501 Squadron, Kinloss.
Shuttleworth Collection, Old Warden. AR501. Built 1942. No. 310 Squadron, Exeter.

MARK VIII
RAF St. Athan, South Wales. MT818. Built 1944. No. 315 Squadron, Burtonwood.

MARK IX
Birmingham Museum of Science and Industry. ML427. Built 1944. No. 3501 Support Unit.
Duxford Airfield, Cambridge. MH 434. Built 1943. No. 222 Squadron, Hornchurch.
RAF St. Athan, South Wales. MH 356. Built 1944. No. 443 Squadron (RCAF), RAF Digby.
Warbirds of Great Britain Ltd, Blackbushe, near Yateley, Hants. NH238. Built 1944. No. 84 Group Support Unit.

MARK XI
Castle Donington. PL983. Built 1944. No. 1 Pilot's Pool, Benson.

MARK XIV
Classic Air Displays, Elstree. NH904. Built 1945. No. 414 Squadron.
RAF Aerospace Museum, Cosford. MT847. Built 1945. No. 6 Motor Unit, Brize Norton.
Rolls Royce Ltd, Castle Donington. RM689. Built 1944. Air Fighting Development Unit, Wittering.

Warbirds of Great Britain Ltd, Blackbushe, near Yateley, Hants. MV293. Built 1945. No. 33 Motor Unit, Lyneham.

Warbirds of Great Britain Ltd, Blackbushe, near Yateley, Hants. SM832. Built 1945. No. 222 Motor Unit, High Ercall.

Whitehall Theatre of War, London. MV370. Built 1945. No. 39 Motor Unit, Colerne.

MARK XVI

R. J. Mitchell Memorial Museum, Hanley, Stoke-on-Trent. RW388. Built 1945. No. 667 Squadron.

RAF Bentley Priory, Middlesex. SL574. Built 1945. No. 6 Motor Unit, Brize Norton.

RAF Biggin Hill, Kent. SL674. Built 1945. No. 501 (County of Gloucester) Squadron, Filton.

RAF Central Flying School, Leeming. TE356. No. 695 Squadron.

RAF Coltishall, Norfolk. SL542. Built 1945. No. 595 Squadron.

RAF Credenhill, Hereford. TE392. Built 1945. No. 126 Squadron.

RAF Exhibition Flight, Abingdon. TE311. Built 1945. No. 39 Motor Unit, Colerne.

RAF Exhibition Flight, Abingdon. TB382. Built 1944. No. 602 (County of Glasgow) Squadron, Ludham, Norfolk.

RAF Leuchars, Fife. TB252. Built 1945. No. 329 Squadron.

RAF Manston, Kent. TB752. Built 1945. No. 66 Squadron, Linton upon Ouse.

RAF Northolt, Middlesex. TE476. Built 1945. No. 33 Motor Unit, Lyneham.

RAF Sealand, Clwyd. TD248. Built 1945. No. 695 Squadron.

RAF Turnhouse, Edinburgh. RW393. Built 1945. No. 203 Advanced Flying School.

RAF Uxbridge. RW382. Built 1945. No. 6 Motor Unit, Brize Norton.

Royal Scottish Museum of Flight, East Fortune, North Berwick. TE462. Built 1945. No. 33 Motor Unit, Lyneham.

Ulster Folk and Transport Museum, Holywood, Co. Down. TE184. Built 1945. No. 6 Motor Unit, Brize Norton.

Warbirds of Great Britain Ltd, Blackbushe, near Yateley, Hants. RW386. Built 1945. No. 604 (County of Middlesex) Squadron.

MARK XVIII

Warbirds of Great Britain Ltd, Blackbushe, near Yateley, Hants. SM969. Built 1945. No. 6 Motor Unit, Brize Norton.

MARK XIX

RAF Battle of Britain Memorial Flight, Coningsby. PM631. Built 1945. No. 6 Motor Unit, Brize Norton.

RAF Battle of Britain Memorial Flight, Coningsby. PS853. Built 1945. Central Photographic Reconnaissance Unit, Benson.

RAF Benson, Oxfordshire. PM 651. Built 1945. No. 6 Motor Unit, Brize Norton.

RAF Brawdy, Dyfed. PS915. Built 1945. No. 541 Squadron.

MARK XXI

RAF Locking, Avon. LA198. Built 1944. No. 1 Squadron, Manston.

RAF Wittering. LA255. Built 1945. No. 1. (Fighter) Squadron.

Vickers Ltd, South Marston. LA226. Built 1945. No. 91 (Nigerian) Squadron.

MARK XXII

RAF Abingdon, Oxfordshire. PK624. Built 1945. No. 33 Motor Unit, Lyneham.

RAF Binbrook, Lincolnshire. PK664. Built 1945. No. 615 (County of Surrey) Squadron.

MARK XXIV

R. J. Mitchell Hall, Spitfire Museum, Southampton. PK 683. Built 1946. No. 47 Motor Unit, Sealand.

RAF Museum, Hendon. PK724. Built 1946. No. 33 Motor Unit, Lyneham.